*More Precious
than Gold*

More Precious than Gold

The Fiery Trial of a Family's Faith

John and Brenda Vaughn

Fleming H. Revell
A Division of Baker Book House Co
Grand Rapids, Michigan 49516

Published by Fleming H. Revell
a division of Baker Book House Company
P.O. Box 6287, Grand Rapids, MI 49516-6287

Third printing, March 1996

Printed in the United States of America

Library of Congress Cataloging-in-Publication Data

Vaughn, John, 1948–
    More precious than gold : the fiery trial of a family's faith / John and Brenda Vaughn.
       p.   cm.
    ISBN 0-8007-5519-7
    1. Vaughn, John, 1948–   . 2. Baptists—United States—Clergy—Biography. 3. Vaughn, Brenda. 4. Vaughn, Rebecca Morel. 5. Burns and scalds—Religious aspects—Christianity. 6. Burns and scalds in children—Religious aspects—Christianity. 7. Suffering—Religious aspects—Christianity. 8. Providence and governance of God.
    I. Vaughn, Brenda. II. Title.
BX6495.V35A3 1994
248.8'6'0922—dc20   93-37584
[B]

To
JIM and PAT
who helped sweep up the ashes

Contents

Preface

And thou shalt remember all the way which the LORD thy God
led thee these forty years in the wilderness, to humble thee, and
to prove thee, to know what was in thine heart, whether thou
wouldest keep his commandments, or no.

Deuteronomy 8:2

The two balancing truths of real-
ity on earth are God's sovereignty and man's responsibility. One cannot cancel out the other, for it is the Sovereign God who holds man
responsible. This is a story of these two truths and the lessons that
taught us this balance. Although we can do things contrary to the
will of God, nothing can happen to us contrary to the will of God.

Brenda and I can see many reasons that God might have wanted
to break us: We were proud, willful, rebellious, and unusable to God.
But Becky was only two years old when her life was unalterably
changed. Her hope for a normal life was taken from her in an instant.
Did she deserve such a loss? No one would be callous enough to say
that. Was God powerless to prevent this tragedy? No, not the omnipotent God.

Brokenness teaches us to see with the eye of faith what can never
be seen in the circumstances; it teaches us to see our lives in the context of eternity. A. W. Tozer says it far better.

If God has singled you out to be a special object of His grace you may
expect Him to honor you with stricter discipline and greater suffering than less favored ones are called upon to endure.

9

If God sets out to make you an unusual Christian He is not likely to be as gentle as He is usually pictured by the popular teachers. A sculptor does not use a manicure set to reduce the rude, unshapely marble to a thing of beauty. The saw, the hammer and the chisel are cruel tools, but without them the rough stone must remain forever formless and unbeautiful.

To do His supreme work of grace within you He will take from your heart everything you love most. Everything you trust in will go from you. Piles of ashes will lie where your most precious treasures used to be.

Thus you will learn what faith is; you will find out the hard way, but the only way open to you, that true faith lies in the will, that the joy unspeakable of which the apostle speaks is not itself faith but a slow-ripening fruit of faith. You will learn, too, that present spiritual joys may come and go as they will without altering your spiritual status or in any way affecting your position as a true child of the heavenly Father.

Then you will also learn, probably to your astonishment, that it is possible to live in all good conscience before God and men and still feel nothing of the 'peace and joy' you hear talked about so much by immature Christians![1]

The author of these words was explaining the wonderful truth of Hebrews 12:11, "No chastening for the present seemeth to be joyous, but grievous: nevertheless afterward it yieldeth the peaceable fruit of righteousness." Tozer understood the balance between sovereignty and responsibility. Those who are learning it are learning to leave God's business to God while diligently standing by their own responsibilities, regardless of how they feel.

There is a priceless oneness between a husband and wife that can never be achieved through a mere agreement. This oneness is something God gives to a couple, not something they achieve on their own. We vow "for better or worse," but we mean "for better." "In sickness or in health," we say, and although an occasional cold is expected, we never plan on major physical trauma.

Sadly, many couples never know this oneness. There is a kind of emotional divorce today where two people stay together but live separate lives. They have common property and a common name. They have borne children together. They live their lives eating at the same table, sleeping in the same bed, making payments on adjoining grave plots. They are one in name, but not in fact.

There is open strife among others, those who do not divorce, either legally or emotionally, but who simply cannot get along. For them, life is one long struggle of constantly pressuring their partner to keep the terms of the contract—to live up to their expectations, a desperate longing for the other to be the partner of their dreams. They lead two lives: their everyday life of duty and frustration, and the imaginary life toward which they strive—the dream, the fantasy, the hope that someday their partner will become what they have always wanted.

Becky's story begins here but will have to be told in full later; perhaps she will tell it herself. This is the story of how God made a marriage from the ashes of selfishness. It is the story of a fire God used to reveal our pride—to humble us so that He could lift us up. Brenda and I will be sharing things that not only were difficult to learn, but are difficult to talk about. We have tried our best to tell this story without being vague, but also without unnecessarily embarrassing others involved who may not desire the transparency and accountability required of us.

Just as burn victims are among the most vulnerable of all the injured—to touch them even in compassion is to cause pain—so the frustrated marriage partner is vulnerable too. This book is offered as another painful dressing change for the wounded, another step in the healing process. Healing brings hope, but it is lengthy, costly, and sometimes, even when successful, unable to bring about a complete recovery. There will be scars. Marital health, like physical health, is not a thing to be achieved with early effort and enjoyed at leisure. It is a lifelong project.

For those who are trying to rebuild a marriage, begin a marriage, or just keep growing together, our prayer is that as we go through the pain of removing our own bandages here in this story, you will begin to see the hope we are seeing: "That the trial of your faith, being much more precious than of gold that perisheth, though it be tried with fire, might be found unto praise and honour and glory at the appearing of Jesus Christ" (1 Peter 1:7). We pray that you may be able to say with Job, "He knoweth the way that I take: when he hath tried me, I shall come forth as gold" (Job 23:10). A scriptural marriage or a truly broken and useful life is like gold—very, very expensive. Our prayer is that as we bare our hearts, others will come to see that it is truly more precious than gold.

Acknowledgments

Debts of gratitude are never paid; they are merely acknowledged. Our prayer is that the debts we owe to others will be paid in eternal dividends to the accounts of those who have invested in our lives and in this story. There are doctors, nurses, teachers, family, and friends so numerous it would be impossible to name all who have contributed to the lessons shared here.

The writing would never have begun without the encouragement of hundreds of friends who have heard the story and urged us to share it in print. The initial outline dates back to a friendship with Richard Peck nearly fifteen years ago. Kathy Martin typed our immature attempts to tell the story and thereby helped us decide to wait for another decade until the lessons were more fully understood.

Betty Day and Elaine Hundt both contributed many hours of work in the early stages of writing. Elaine's gracious translation of John's illegible handwriting made everyone else's tasks possible. The lion's share of manuscript production is the fruit of Julie Wingate's gifts. Without her skills on the computer and her knowledge of writing and book production, the story might never have been sent to the publisher in acceptable form.

Dr. Grace Collins taught us the equivalent of several graduate hours in grammar and style during the numerous drafts of the manuscript, but had we known what an excellent editor Mary Suggs of Fleming H. Revell was, we could have sent the project in much earlier. Thanks also to editorial director Bill Petersen for his patience and helpful guidance. These and many others played an important part in the actual production of this book.

Thanks to all who read the manuscript and made helpful suggestions. Special thanks to all who will recognize their own words and ideas that we have come to think of as our own. It is not our intention to claim credit for that which we have received from others but have forgotten exactly when or where.

Far beyond the practical help of so many, there is a deeper debt we owe: to the people of Faith Baptist Church who have, by their teachable hearts and sweet submission, given a credibility to our ministry that is beyond our own accomplishment; to our parents and siblings who have shared in the story far more than most will ever realize; to our five children who have sweetly and patiently waited for their parents to work their way through struggles that many parents have resolved long before their children are old enough to know; and especially to our loving Lord and Savior, who knows all the things we could never tell in writing, but loves us anyway.

Part One

The Smelting Process

Beloved, think it not strange concerning the fiery trial which is to try you, as though some strange thing happened unto you: But rejoice, inasmuch as ye are partakers of Christ's sufferings; that, when his glory shall be revealed, ye may be glad also with exceeding joy.

1 Peter 4:12–13

Chapter One

But we have this treasure in earthen vessels, that the excellency of the power may be of God, and not of us.

2 Corinthians 4:7

MONDAY
MAY 22, 1978, 8:30 P.M.

The children were asleep in the back seat. They had been so excited about the new toys we had bought for the trip. With all the losses they had to deal with, my heart was broken for them that they had nothing to play with in the long days of waiting that lay ahead. Now, the stress of the last two days was taking its toll; and though we had talked about having a good time in the car, I was thankful that they were asleep. I reached for the radio, then decided against it to keep from waking them. Debbie was leaning against the center armrest and Johnny was leaning against her. I looked to see that their seat belts were fastened, then adjusted the rearview mirror so the setting sun behind me wouldn't glare into my eyes.

I've never been to Charleston. No, there was one time when I was in the service. We went to the Navy base exchange there since the Air Force base at Myrtle Beach did not have a good selection of fishing gear. I thought about Gary and Dara. It was their idea to take that trip. Gary not only led me to Christ but has kept in touch ever since. What will they think when they hear about the accident?

I was tired too, and afraid I would fall asleep. The worst wreck I had ever had was in the late '60s. I'd fallen asleep on the interstate coming back from Cumberland College from a two-day visit to see Brenda in summer school.

I couldn't bear to think about what lay ahead; but the more I tried to keep the speed down, the more I became bored and got sleepy. I prayed for God to help me drive safely. I shook my head sharply and tried to focus my thoughts on something specific; almost immediately I found myself remembering a hot, humid night in Thailand—the night I had accepted the Lord as my Savior. What was it I'd said that night? For the first time, I had approached God with a correct understanding of whom I was addressing. The intensity of that knowledge reduced my selfish plans for my life to proper perspective. "Lord, it looks like things are changing," I had begun. "Becoming a pilot doesn't seem so important—"

A brilliant glare in my eyes made me swerve sharply, yanking my thoughts back to the road. *Was that a horn, or just the bright lights? A truck probably. Better keep my eyes on the road.* But my mind returned to the same train of thought. Things sure *did* change. And they've *kept* changing—awfully fast. I had always wanted to be a writer—I wondered if God was giving me something worth writing about.

It seemed impossible that Saturday had been only two days before.

Saturday
May 20, 1978

We had been playing ball in the front yard. The Merkles had come to Greenville to interview for a teaching job at Bob Jones University. Their kids and ours were batting the ball and running the imaginary bases. Two-year-old Becky was having a great time. She cheered and clapped her hands as Johnny ran.

When the Merkles came home, we made sure they had all they needed in their room. That night we talked of another visit they needed to make; they planned to take their children with them. We enjoyed a meal together.

Our children were nine, seven, and two, and we had a twelve-year-old guest, the daughter of a couple whom we had encouraged to attend the couples' retreat at the Wilds Christian Camp.

We didn't miss Becky at the table until I smelled the gasoline. She had gone to the utility room. There was a gas can near the door to the back steps. This was something new; I never put dangerous items there, but today I felt it important to put it inside away from some neighborhood boys who had gotten into some old paint cans at the vacant house next door.

We would be moving in just a few days, and I had sold most of the lawn equipment I had used in my yard business—I had cut grass to pay bills while finishing college. I didn't have a single mower left; and if I was going to borrow a mower, I certainly wasn't going to borrow the gas! When I brought it home that morning, the boys had seen me put it under the shrubs by the back door.

This will never do, I had thought as I placed it inside. Now, I found Becky beside the can, prying at the lid with her tiny fingers. Seven years of working around aircraft had taught me the dangers of flammable liquids. I scolded Becky and told her, "Don't touch the gasoline."

I tightened the lid and explained to my wife that Becky had knocked the can over and a few drops had leaked out, but I had cleaned it up and would put the can back outside when I got home from visiting in the hospital that evening.

"Could we put it up on the shelf?" she asked.

"No, Honey, we shouldn't put it near the heat of the water heater or the dryer. I'll get it outside as soon as I get home. Just keep the door to the utility room closed. It should be okay."

After the meal, the Merkles left to visit some friends. I told my wife I needed to go by the hospital to see Mrs. Robertson and her new baby, and then I would stop by our realtor's home. I wanted to make sure everything had gone well with the sale of our home to ensure that we would be able to move into the new house on June 1—just ten days away. In a couple of hours I was saying good-bye at my last visit. On my way to the car I realized that I hadn't finished the bulletin for Sunday morning.

Oh, great. That will take another hour, and it's nearly nine o'clock.

* * *

Saturday
May 20, 8:50 p.m.

John will be home any minute. I finally had all the ingredients to make one of our favorite desserts. I had bought Jell-O one week, the cake mix another week, the cans of cherries the next week, then the whipped topping. *It will be perfect for Sunday dinner tomorrow. We're having company!*

The children had taken their baths. Debbie, who was nine, and Kathy, our twelve-year-old visitor, were playing in Debbie's bedroom. Johnny, seven years old, was sitting on the couch in the living room reading a book. As I stirred the cake, Becky wandered through the kitchen, dragging her blanket as she always did. I wondered if the blanket was clean. It was hard to get it away from her to wash it. When I thought she wouldn't miss it, I'd put it in the washing machine. Often, it would no sooner get wet than she would discover it was gone. Then she'd stand in front of the washer saying she wanted her "bynie."

Only once did I take her to the babysitter's and forget to bring her blanket. "I'll be glad to go back home for it," I said.

"No, that's okay. We'll make it," the sitter assured me. When I picked up Becky a few hours later, the babysitter told me wearily that she had made a big mistake. Becky had cried the whole time.

Thank goodness she can't lose her thumb. She'll always have that with her. She was the only one of our children who had ever sucked her thumb or had an attachment to something like her blanket. It was so cute. Often when she was sucking her thumb I'd ask, "Becky, is that good? Can I try that?"

She would pull her wrinkled thumb out of her mouth and offer it to me so that I could have the same pleasure she did from it. She was so content and had brought such joy to our lives. I smiled as I watched her leave the room again, and she smiled at me with her sweet little smile. I turned back to my cake. Saturday night had always been a special time.

When John and I were in college, skating parties were held at school on Saturday nights. The oldest gym had been turned into a skating rink. I would watch John glide around the rink, and I wished he would skate with me. One time he did. My heart pounded, my hands got sweaty, and I wondered if he had noticed. After that I never wanted to go home on the weekends because there was always a chance I might be able to skate with him again. After we were married, but not yet living for the Lord, Saturday nights had a completely different meaning: sometimes partying, sometimes having friends over to play games.

But now that we were in the ministry, Saturday night was a very busy time—time for getting things ready for Sunday morning, making sure the children's shoes were shined and shirts ironed. My biggest job was to get all possible Sunday dinner preparations done ahead of time. John would be home in just a few minutes, and I had allowed the children to stay up a little late to say goodnight to him. It was almost nine o'clock.

Where is Becky? Being busy in the kitchen, I hadn't seen her for a couple of minutes. Suddenly the nauseating smell of gasoline overpowered the sweet aroma from the cake I had just put in the oven. *Oh, no. I left the utility door open. John told me to be careful when he put the gas can in there.* Somehow, Becky had loosened the lid and turned the can over. The lid was off, and the gasoline now flowed out onto the floor.

What a mess! I've got to get this up; this is not safe!

Just then Debbie came into the kitchen. "Debbie," I ordered, "you and Kathy run to the bathroom and get me as many towels as you can. I've got to get this up. Run! Run!"

They dashed to the linen closet down the hall, and I reached for Becky, who was now sitting in a puddle of gasoline. Suddenly, there was a bright flash—immediately we were engulfed in flames! There was no place to turn. The fire was everywhere! I couldn't see Becky! My clothes were on fire! It happened so suddenly. I couldn't believe it at first.

This isn't happening. This is a dream. I've got to wake up! It was no dream, yet there was no pain, no panic. Just a feeling of unbelief. Becky was screaming helplessly. In an instant I knew I had to get Becky out of the fire. It was not an instinctive act but a rational choice. *She's so precious to us!* From the very beginning, we knew that she had come from the Lord. *If I don't do something, she'll die. I'm the only adult in the house and the only one who can do anything.* The Lord helped me act decisively with my next thought. *If she dies, it will kill her father; I'd rather die anyway than let her burn to death.*

Bending down into the flames, I scooped up Becky with my left arm. The back door was stuck! I tugged, jerked, twisted, then frantically pulled at it. Finally it gave way and opened. The neighbors had heard the explosion and came running to help. I was trying to beat out the flames that covered my little daughter from head to foot. She clung to my right shoulder, screaming in fear and pain.

Mr. Blocker, a neighbor, struggled to grab Becky away from me and roll her on the ground. I was too confused to understand what he wanted to do. Then I found myself also rolling on the ground until the flames were out. Unbelievably, I still felt no pain. I looked up at the sky. It was clear, and the stars were so bright. *I might die. This might be it.*

I'd always thought I would be afraid to die. When we moved to Greenville, I had been scared because there were rumors of a high crime rate. I was afraid for my husband to leave me in the car when he went into a store, because I thought somebody might try to hurt me. For a while I had been preoccupied with the thought of dying. I didn't dread the destination—I knew that Christ had saved me—but death itself had scared me whenever I thought about it. Now, with the bright stars above and the cold ground beneath me, a sense of peace and sadness came over me. *I won't see my children grow up. I might be with the Lord in just a few minutes.* I didn't expect any great change to occur. That thought was very comforting.

The flames were out and I still felt no pain, so I staggered to my feet to find the children. The front yard was full of people. Fire trucks, ambulances, and police cars with lights flashing were closing in. I searched for Debbie and Johnny. I thought I remembered yelling, "Everybody out!" before I left the utility room, but I didn't know if they had heard me.

Every mother's nightmare was coming true for me. What would I do if all my children were in a life-threatening situation? I had saved only one. That's all I could do—she was the one right in front of me, in the flames. I had to get her out. I tried to warn the others. *Oh, God, don't let them be in the house!*

Then I saw them. There, huddled with a neighbor, were Debbie and Johnny. They looked at me with huge, frightened eyes. I ran toward them, not realizing how horrifying my appearance must have been to them. My skin was charred and bloody. My dress was tattered and matted with grass and debris. My blonde hair was black with ashes and soot.

"Johnny, are you all right? Are you okay?" I pleaded as he backed rapidly away.

"Mommy, is that you? Is that you, Mommy?" he cried.

My neighbor, Carolyn Millett, realized his fear. "They're both fine, Brenda," she assured me. "Don't worry. I'll take care of them." Both children were crying. I looked at Debbie and she looked at me, but Carolyn was taking them away. "I'm going to take them to my house. Don't worry!" She hurried the children away.

An EMS worker was holding my arm.

"How is Becky?" I asked. "Is she going to live?"

"She's still alive, and she's crying. That's a good sign."

"Where is she? I have to be with her."

"We'll get to that in a little while. We need to take care of you right now." He was so kind, so reassuring. I had to trust him.

Soon I was lying down, partially covered with a sheet. Then I began to feel the pain—dull at first, then almost unbearable. Above the pain of my body, I heard another painful sound. I thought I could hear Becky screaming, "Mommy! Mommy!" But there was nothing I could do. They wouldn't let me move.

"Oh, Becky!" I cried.

"She's in the ambulance, Mrs. Vaughn. They're taking her to the hospital now."

I resigned myself to that and began to wonder where John was.

"Mrs. Vaughn, we're going to have to cut off your clothes and jewelry."

They can't do that! I'm a pastor's wife! "Please be discreet," I told the paramedic, "I'm a pastor's wife." I still had no idea what I looked like.

"Caucasian female," I heard one of them say. "Approximately twenty-seven years old."

"Twenty-nine," I said, feeling I needed to be honest.

* * *

The ten-minute ride home went quickly. I focused entirely on the bulletin and made sure that all the planning and layout were in mind so all I would have to do was cut the stencil to take to church early the next morning.

I pulled into my neighborhood. Down the tree-lined street, it was three blocks to East Belvedere Road. There was a deputy's car— the road was blocked. I thought I would have to go around, but he saw my turn signal and motioned for me to stop. I rolled down the window to see what the trouble could be.

"May I pass?" I asked. "I live on this street."

"What number?" he said.

"Two fourteen."

"Are you the preacher?"

"Yes, sir."

"Yes, quick, go ahead."

Almost in slow motion, I turned down my street, down the hill to where I saw a fire truck, an EMS truck, two police cars with lights flashing, and quite a commotion. I don't remember parking the car, getting out, or running into the yard, but I was standing there with my neighbor, Perry, from across the street who was holding me by the shoulders.

I don't remember if he said anything; I remember only my own question. "What happened?" I asked. "Who's hurt?"

"Brenda and Becky," he replied. "There's been a fire, and Becky's gone to the hospital. Brenda's around here. Come with me."

His pastor was there. I had never met him before.

Does he live nearby? I wondered. *Who are all these people? Where's the dog?*

"Perry, where are Debbie and Johnny?"

"At my house," he said. "They're fine."

Brenda was lying on the ground, partially covered with a sheet. Two uniformed men were working with her. I knelt beside her.

"Don't touch her," one of them ordered.

She was horribly burned. Her hair was matted and scorched. Her shoulders were bleeding. There were bloodstains on the sheet that covered her.

"Honey!" I cried.

"Oh, Honey, it hurts," she said. "I got Becky out."

"What happened?" I asked, choking back tears.

We both said it at the same time. "The gas can!"

"She must have gotten it open," my wife said. "I didn't see her in the utility room. I was baking a cake for tomorrow. Maybe the heat from the oven, or a spark."

"We'll talk about it later," I said. "Let's pray."

* * *

When I opened my eyes again, John was there. I could hear his voice. He stood beside me, then he knelt. When I saw him, I began to cry.

"The Lord is in control here, Honey. We have to trust Him."

I was glad John was there. I was beginning to lose any strength I had and was very glad to be able to depend on him.

* * *

After we prayed, the men continued to work, cutting away Brenda's rings, struggling to get her ready for the trip to the hospital. While they finished, I ran across the street. Debbie and Johnny were terrified. They stood in the door of the neighbor's home. I knelt with them to pray briefly and hugged them.

"You'll have to stay here," I said. "I'll be back as soon as I can. I've got to go to the hospital with Mommy."

"I got out the window, Daddy," Debbie said.

"I'm so scared," Johnny cried.

"Will Mommy be okay?" they asked. "Will Becky be okay?"

As they sobbed into my shoulder, a deputy quickly grabbed my arm. "We've got to go, *now.*"

Nodding to the deputy, I said to the kids, "Don't worry. I'll be back. Don't worry, just pray." I pulled away as they clung to me; then they turned to hold each other.

The doors were already latched on the back of the EMS truck. I jumped in the front seat, looking back to see if I could talk to Brenda. She couldn't hear me. The cab was sealed off from the back of the truck.

* * *

I couldn't see John, but I knew he was in the ambulance, too. As we raced to the hospital, I tried to speak to him again.

"Honey, do you think I'm going to make it? Honey, do you think I'm going to be all right?" John had always been my source of strength. He'd always been able to fix my problems. Somehow I thought he would know the answers to these questions, too.

But the paramedic next to me was the one who answered. "Mrs. Vaughn, he can't hear you. He's up front. I'm Veda. I'm a Christian. Can I pray with you?" What a comfort that was to me! I later found out that was Veda's first night on EMS duty. The Lord had put her in that ambulance for me. It was no coincidence. The Lord had known what was coming and had prepared a friend to be there for me.

Her presence reassured me that the Lord knew what was happening. He too might have wept that night as He watched Becky loosen the lid on the gas can, but He knew what was needed in our lives. For me, at that very moment, the message came through loud and clear. God loves me! I know that He will do only what is best for me.

* * *

"Please fasten your seat belt, sir," the driver said as he pulled onto the street.

I kept praying, "Oh God, don't let them die. I love You, Lord. Please help me to be strong."

I needed to do something, somehow, right there to declare that we were going to honor God through this, no matter what. I took out my pocket calendar. May 20, 1978—all I could write was "I love You, Lord."

Chapter Two

We are troubled on every side, yet not distressed; we are perplexed, but not in despair; persecuted, but not forsaken; cast down, but not destroyed.

2 Corinthians 4:8–9

A sheriff's deputy drove ahead of the ambulance. When we reached the city limits, a city police car quickly took over the escort. We were at Greenville General Hospital, six miles from our home, within six minutes. By the time I got out of the ambulance and closed the door behind me, the emergency room workers had placed Brenda on a stretcher, and were heading through the heavy swinging doors. I followed them and looked at the woman behind the desk. Just as I said, "I have insurance," she motioned to me to go through to the emergency room.

There were several small spaces—not actually rooms, but little cubicles divided by curtains. Brenda was already in one of them; I wasn't sure where. I looked around and felt very much out of place.

What can I do? Can I talk to her? What is she thinking? I know she must be scared. Where is Becky? Is she still alive?

A kind woman came up beside me. "Are you Mr. Vaughn?" she asked.

"Yes, I am."

"Come with me. I have a place where you can wait. There is a telephone. You can make any calls you'd like. Would you like a glass of water?"

"No, thanks."

"Well, if I can get you anything, just let me know."

This was strange. I had heard so many stories about the emergency room hassle concerning insurance; yet no one had hassled me. I was not in some uncomfortable place nor treated rudely. We walked to the family room. *Well, this is an* emergency *room,* I thought. In those few minutes, I put the insect bites, high temperatures, toothaches, and other minor injuries that had taken us to the hospital over the years in proper context. The woman closed the door behind me and told me that someone would be in to give me a report on Brenda and Becky as soon as possible.

I sat down to think about whom I should call, but I couldn't get my mind off Brenda and Becky.

Will they wonder where I am?

I didn't know all that had happened that night, but I remembered the scene repeatedly after I pieced it together. Becky had gone to the utility room and had somehow managed to get the gasoline can opened. Evidently she had turned it over. Brenda was startled to see the gasoline flowing into the kitchen. She did not know how easily gasoline could be ignited. She knew it was dangerous and that it would irritate Becky's skin. She knew it needed to be cleaned up immediately. Her first thought was a good one: *Send the kids to the linen closet, get lots of towels, quickly mop up the gasoline, and throw them out the back door. That should prevent danger.*

We would see later from the charred floor that when the gas got close to the heat of the oven, it had ignited, exploding like a bomb. The flames engulfed Becky entirely and Brenda was in flames up to her shoulders. Somehow, probably from a gasoline-soaked towel, Kathy sustained burns on her hands and face, but she was able to get out of the front door quickly.

The flames from the explosion shot through the kitchen door across the living room. Johnny, who was on the couch, immediately escaped out the front door. The flames quickly cut off that door, trapping Debbie in the back of the house. Brenda had taught them what to do in case of emergencies. Debbie quickly knocked the screen out of the window with her brother's ball bat and dropped a few feet to the ground below.

In the inferno off the kitchen, Brenda reached down into the flames and grabbed Becky. With Becky screaming, she embraced her with her left arm, and groped through the flames for the door to the utility room that opened to the outside. I was angry with myself later for not responding to her many requests to fix that door. It always stuck. I meant to get to it; I just never did. Somehow she got the door open. By the time she stumbled down the two concrete steps to the ground below, two of our neighbors were there.

Brenda and Becky were both in flames. Their clothing, their hair, even their flesh was burning. The neighbor man separated them. Brenda rolled on the ground several times to extinguish the flames. The other man rolled Becky on the ground. Her screaming subsided as she passed out. It would be months before she would be fully conscious again.

When Debbie and Johnny saw their mother, they were terrified. Our neighbor took them across the street to her home, where they were when I arrived ten minutes later.

A fire truck from the Gantt Fire Department arrived less than two minutes after the explosion. They extinguished the flames and structural damage to the house was avoided. The EMS trucks were right behind the fire trucks.

I reviewed these events in my mind while I waited in the emergency room, but there were questions I could not answer.

Why? What next? Then I remembered the sermon I had preached on April 23, just a month before. The title was "The Crucible of Christian Suffering." I had taught my congregation about being broken through pain and problems. I had given the invitation that night with these words: "Some of us here may not be willing to allow God to do things in our lives now that will count for eternity. We must make ourselves available for God to use. We must be willing to experience this fiery trial—this smelting process—so that the dross can be burned away and the priceless gold can be seen."

Brenda had stepped down the aisle that night to meet me at the altar. We knew there was much work to be done. We knew that we had not laid a good foundation for our marriage, for our ministry, or for our lives. We committed everything to God and said, in essence, "Lord, do whatever is necessary to be done to make our lives count for Thee."

Is this it? Is this the breaking process? I wondered. I knew God was involved. No, I knew He was in control. *Then we will leave it with Him.*

As I waited there in the family room of the hospital for a seemingly endless hour, I thought back to our afternoon ball game. I remembered Becky clapping her hands, and I remembered her excitement as we cheered for each other. I thought about our church picnic at Timmons Park a few weeks before—how, as I was batting, Becky had called in her sweet little voice, "Daddy!" I had turned to see her pucker her little lips through the chain-link backstop, and I had called "time out" to go back and give her a kiss. I had touched those pudgy, little hands through the fence. "I love you," I had told her.

Becky's eyes twinkled and her chubby little cheeks dimpled into a big grin.

I choked up as I remembered, and I prayed for God to spare my little girl. *Brenda had saved her life.*

"Oh God, spare them both, and ease their pain."

Chapter Three

Always bearing about in the body the dying of the Lord Jesus,
that the life also of Jesus might be made manifest in our body.

2 Corinthians 4:10

SATURDAY, 10:00 P.M.

I was shocked back into reality with the thought that I must contact the family whose daughter, our house guest, had also been burned. Apparently, she had been brought to the hospital in the ambulance with Becky. I made some quick phone calls and got word to the director of the camp where they were. "Their daughter has been injured, I'm not sure how badly. They will need to return to Greenville right away."

I was concerned that all the good we had tried to do for this family would now be undone by this tragedy. Their marriage was in trouble. We had offered to keep their daughter if they would attend a couples' retreat that weekend. Now she was in the hospital.

Will they be bitter, angry at us? Will my insurance cover their expenses as well?

Folks from our church began to arrive. Dr. Walt Handford, our former pastor, and his wife, Libby, walked in. They were so comforting. That was the first in a series of hundreds of lessons on the importance of support from godly friends. I drew strength from Dr.

Handford's strength. Just as they arrived, the nurse told me, "You can see your wife now."

"Will you go with me?" I asked Dr. Handford.

"Sure I will," he said.

We stood there beside the emergency room gurney where my wife lay bleeding under a sterile sheet. It is almost impossible to describe what we saw. I would later learn that Brenda had sustained third-degree burns on 65 percent of her body. She would require extensive skin grafts on her neck, her arms from the shoulders to the fingers, her legs from the thighs to the toes and much of her back, especially the shoulder to which Becky had clung while they escaped the flames. Brenda's scarred and twisted left hand would become a constant reminder of the sacrifice she had made to save Becky's life.

Brenda was awake. "How is Becky?"

"I don't know," I said. "I haven't seen her yet. We'll see her soon."

Brenda looked through her eyes glazed with heavy sedation and recognized Dr. Handford. "Is Mrs. Handford here?" she asked hopefully.

"Yes, she is," Dr. Handford said softly.

"May I see her?" Brenda pleaded.

Dr. Handford slipped away to get Mrs. Handford. I wanted to touch my wife to comfort her, to reassure her of my love, but there was no place to touch her. While third-degree burns covered over half of her body, Brenda's face and shoulders were also covered with bleeding and blistered second-degree burns.

Mrs. Handford was at my side. "I love you, Brenda," she spoke softly.

"Mrs. Handford, is God chastening me?" my wife asked in a groggy voice.

I was shocked at the boldness of her question. I felt guilty. I thought of all those times I had argued with my wife, made accusations and angry threats. I was ashamed of my selfishness—overwhelmed with a sense of indignation at myself. I had so selfishly and for so many years tried to force my wife to be what I had wanted her to be. In this situation, as in so many others, Brenda felt entirely responsible. I remembered saying just a few days before, while chiding her for something she wasn't doing exactly the way I had wanted it done, "What's it going to take to get your attention?" I prayed she wouldn't remember that angry statement now.

"No," Mrs. Handford said, "this isn't chastening."

I wondered at her confidence. Later we would both come to realize that when God communicates through chastening, he communicates clearly. Just as conviction comes, not in a general sense of uneasiness, but in a clear awareness of a specific requirement from God, so too does chastening come, not to those who don't know what God is trying to do, but to those who know but will not obey.

Mrs. Handford comforted Brenda, prayed with her, and gave her reassurance of the Lord's love and the sufficiency of His grace. I had committed Brenda to the Lord and now I prayed for myself. *Will I have the strength that she needs me to have? What about Becky?* I knew that God was giving me an opportunity to learn what faith and trust really mean.

Doctors and nurses, too many people for such a small space, were busily but quietly going about their urgent tasks. A blue curtain divided us from the crisis of some other poor family just a few feet away. Suddenly, the curtain was ripped open. In spite of the gruesome scene of my own wife burned beyond recognition, I turned to see a blood-spattered team of doctors and nurses struggling with an angry, cursing man, whose throat had been deeply slit, apparently in a drunken brawl. I reached for the curtain just as a nurse did. Her face was taut and our eyes met for a fraction of a second before we both closed the curtain together. That brief encounter without words, but with a communication of feelings so intense they couldn't be expressed, was one of a thousand I would experience in the days ahead. There are some situations in life for which there simply are no words. This was one of them.

* * *

I don't remember arriving at the emergency room, but there was a lot of activity, a lot of people shouting orders, a lot of bright lights. I heard a voice, "We'll give you something for the pain in just a moment."

The pain was indescribable at this point, especially in my hands and feet. *Will I lose my hands and feet?* I didn't know then that the pain was a good sign. Third-degree burns don't hurt at all because they kill the skin completely. The less severe burns are the most painful because the nerves are still responsive.

"Mrs. Vaughn? Mrs. Vaughn?" It was the doctor's voice again. "We're going to have to make a long incision down each of your arms and legs to release some pressure. Fluid is building up in your body."

I had begun to swell very badly. Someone had hurriedly hooked up an IV, and they were putting morphine through it. The morphine was beginning to take effect—I felt numb. A warm feeling spread through my body.

"Mrs. Vaughn, we're going to make the first incision now. If you feel anything, please say so."

I felt a little sharp sting every once in a while, not enough to make a fuss about. I fell asleep.

Then John was standing next to me. Mrs. Handford was there, too. As I looked at her, I felt a rush of love and warmth. *She doesn't know how much she has meant to me.* I had not had an easy childhood. I had not known a lot of tender care. I know my parents did their best, but they had so many problems of their own. *I wonder if she has ever had any idea that I used to watch her from a distance in her Sunday school class feeling the warmth that radiated from her. I wonder if she realizes that what I felt from her is what I want my children to feel from me.*

Mrs. Handford, I have never told you what you mean to me, and I want you to know that I love you. I wanted to say it, but I was so confused and sleepy.

She was crying. I too am a pastor's wife, and I can imagine how I would feel if I was called into a situation like that. I felt myself looking to her again for reassurance. *I know I haven't been living the way a dedicated Christian ought to live. I struggle with too many things. I'm basically easygoing—live today, worry about tomorrow later. I'm lazy and undisciplined. I would rather depend on John than on God. I know there are problems that I haven't been working on. . . . Is God punishing me for not being serious with Him?* "Mrs. Handford, is God chastising me?"

I didn't hear her answer. I was floating in and out of consciousness. I heard voices speaking to each other, rather than to me. People seemed to be hurrying in all directions, doing all kinds of things. Then I realized that I was no longer in the emergency room, but in the Intensive Care Unit. Under strong medication, my world narrowed down to just my bed and a few faces hovering above me. I struggled to open my eyes from time to time. I saw John. I asked for a drink, but all that came to quench my thirst was ice chips.

* * *

The shock was setting in. Brenda was drifting in and out of consciousness as I wandered around the corridors trying to get back to the family room. My feet were heavy; I needed something to lean on. I'm not sure when he came, but Pastor Handford was again at my side. He looked at me with the love of a pastor, and our spirits met. It was one of those times that perhaps only pastors feel. It was as though God had sent him at that particular moment—not a minute before, and not a minute later. Before either of us could speak, a nurse asked, "Would you like to see your daughter now?"

"I'll go with you, John," Pastor Handford said.

I don't know where the words came from, but I heard myself say, "Pastor, God knows what we need." What I meant was "Yes, I want you to go with me, and I am trying to trust the Lord."

We walked into another little space with blue-curtained walls. We could still hear the curses of the angry man, the terse commands of the doctors, and the dutiful responses of the nurses. Becky lay on a gurney, partially covered with a sterile sheet. She was unconscious. The little blond ringlets encircling her precious face were gone. The gray-brown mat of singed hair was the first thing I noticed.

She was unconscious, but her eyes were open. Then I noticed the swelling in her face. There was not much bleeding, but the soft pink face with the dimpled smile was now a blackened leather mask. The corners of her mouth were split deeply into her cheeks. The corners of her eyes and nostrils were split as well. Her arms, extended by her sides, revealed the swelling of her upper body. An IV bottle dripped slowly into a tube that disappeared beneath the sheet, and another tube went into a nostril. What was apparently oxygen was flowing through a tracheostomy in her throat. These plastic intrusions into her little life brought no comfort, just the cold, clinical reality of survival.

I fell to my knees beside the gurney. Pastor Handford knelt beside me, his arm around my shoulder as he prayed. For the first time in this horrible evening, I could not hold back the tears. I prayed through deep sobs of grief as I asked for God's will to be done for Becky, for His grace to strengthen me. I realized that nothing would ever be the same.

Then, there was a strange sense of reassurance as I looked again at Becky beneath that sheet. The bloodstains were spreading slowly, and the movement of her labored breathing helped me to know there was a struggle going on. God was in control. Though I was powerless to intervene, it wasn't over yet.

We had to leave. Becky would be taken to the Intensive Care Unit, I was told. My wife was going to x-ray, and then she too would be taken to the Intensive Care Unit.

"Some people want to see you. Then someone will be glad to show you to the ICU waiting room," a helpful woman said.

As we stood by the nurses' desk in the emergency room, Pastor Handford took me by the shoulders, looked straight into my eyes, and said to me in a firm but loving voice, "John, God was not taken by surprise tonight. He was not looking over the battlements of heaven in helpless wonder when the fire broke out. He was there, and He is here."

I didn't answer, but I thought, *Why yes, of course. Yes, that's right. I know that, and that's exactly what I needed to hear.*

Very well, I thought, *if I'm on trial for my faith, then I'll testify of my faith!*

There was a group of my church people waiting for me in the hall. Several others whom I didn't know were there. A woman asked, "Are you the young preacher whose family was burned?"

"Yes, ma'am," I uttered.

"Well, bless your heart. Is there anything we can do?"

Am I supposed to know her, I wondered? "Do you know the Lord Jesus?" I asked, obedient to my recent vow.

"Oh yes," she said.

"Then please pray for us," I said. I didn't think of myself as proud, but I was glad that I had the presence of mind to say that. *Yes, that should have been said,* I was sure.

One of my church members introduced me to a man named Frank. "He's from the sheriff's department, Pastor. He was at the house taking pictures, but he has something he wants to tell you."

"Yes sir, what is it?" I asked. Was it about Kathy? Was there a problem, a liability?

"Mr. Vaughn, I'm a Shriner," he said. "Have you heard of our children's hospitals?"

"Why yes," I replied. "There is one here in town, isn't there?"

"Yes," he said, "but that's an orthopedic hospital. We also have three burns hospitals. If you would like to get Becky into one of our hospitals, just say the word, and we'll take care of it."

I didn't know what to say. I had just made up my mind to act like a preacher through this thing, to take a right stand for the Lord, and now I was forced to make a decision on the spot about whether to accept help from the Shriners. *Aren't they part of the Masons? Wasn't there something questionable about the Masons? Don't they have to take some sort of un-Biblical vows? No, I can't do this.*

"Thank you," I responded "I don't know; I'm not sure what the future holds. I'm not sure what's going to happen. It's too early."

"Well then, take my card. If you want to talk about it further, give me a call, please, anytime."

I could see he meant it. This man really wanted to help. I learned later that before he had left my house, a man from my church had addressed the issue of Masonry with him. They had disagreed. I wondered later if Frank was thinking at that moment that I didn't appreciate his offer, and that I had been thinking what in fact I had been thinking. But there were other reasons why Becky needed to stay in Greenville. Her mother, too, was burned. I couldn't separate them. They would both be in the hospital. *Let's keep them together. The doctor will tell me what to do.* These were my thoughts as we worked our way out of the crowded hall, shook hands with those who had come to encourage us, and said good-bye before I tried to find my way to the ICU waiting room.

Chapter Four

For we which live are alway delivered unto death for Jesus' sake, that the life also of Jesus might be made manifest in our mortal flesh.

2 Corinthians 4:11

SATURDAY, 11:45 P.M.

Two of the men from my church stayed with me at the hospital that night. I had worked part-time with Kelly at United Parcel Service for over a year before I had come to pastor Faith Baptist Church. Al and I had been together for years. We had been stationed together at Myrtle Beach Air Force Base. We had both been in Thailand. Al had been at the missionary's home the night I was saved. Now he was out of the Air Force. He had come back to Greer, just a few miles north of Greenville, and was a member of my church. My two friends located the intensive care waiting room and led me there. Later that night, Kelly went out to get me a razor, a toothbrush, and some other items to freshen up. Al also was a true friend, a man of few words but a man whose quiet presence gave me the reassurance I needed through the difficult night.

The emergency room doctor who had taken Brenda to ICU wanted to talk to me. "Mr. Vaughn, do you have any questions?" he asked.

"Just give it to me straight, doctor. The Lord is giving me strength. I suppose I need to know what we're in for."

"Well," he said, "your wife is going to be in the hospital for awhile."

He saw in my facial expression that I wanted to know how long that meant. "Two, maybe three months at least," he declared.

I thought I was ready to hear the report, but a three-month hospital stay was beyond my comprehension.

"She seems to have been in good health when she was hurt," he went on. "She had a fall of some sort; that's why we sent for x-rays. No broken bones, as far as we know at this time. Her vital signs are fairly good, but she's been burned pretty severely, well over half of her body." It was, in fact, 65 percent third-degree burns, another 20 percent first- and second-degree burns.

The doctor briefly explained that a third-degree burn is a burn that goes all the way through the skin. A first-degree burn is like a blister or a bad sunburn—a superficial wound that will heal fairly well without scarring. A second-degree burn is deeper, very painful, since the nerves are involved. Grafting is not necessary, but there is some scarring. Second-degree burns are very slow to heal, and there is always a possibility of infection.

"But third-degree burns," he explained, "require the replacement of the tissue entirely. The skin will die. A third-degree burn cannot heal without a skin graft. Sometimes adjoining skin will granulate into the wound and cover it over with scar tissue, but in large areas skin grafting is the only alternative. It takes time. There are a number of dangers."

He explained that the initial crisis would last about seventy-two hours while the blood gases would be evaluated regularly and every attempt would be made to stabilize her vital signs. Then a longer period of danger would occur when topical infections posed the greatest threat to life—when necrotic, or dead, skin would be removed through a process called debridement. If the vital signs were stable and no serious infections occurred, grafting could begin in a couple of weeks. Then it would become a matter of allowing the grafts to heal and going through therapy.

"All of this will be explained in greater detail later," he said. The doctor ended his lengthy and somewhat technical report on my wife with these words, "Although she has a very serious injury and will be in very grave danger for quite some time, I am confident. She should make it."

I sensed he wanted to stop his report right there, but I had to know. I could see from his face that he knew he had to tell me. "What about Becky?" I urged him on.

He paused to draw a long breath; a longer sigh followed. Looking at his clipboard he said, "It's hard to say." Before I could insist on more information, he added, "Her burn is almost total. Quite a problem keeping her stable. Her lungs may be burned."

I would later understand what that meant: she wasn't able to breathe on her own, her heartbeat was erratic, and all of her vital signs showed her to be very near death.

"Doctor," I pressed, "if you were to tell me in terms of chances, what would her chances be?"

Looking into my eyes, he simply said, "Less than one percent."

Although I already suspected, it was like a fist in my stomach as I heard these words. I swallowed hard and tried to nod my head. This man was telling me that Becky was going to die.

I felt sorry for him as he walked away. Though this was my wife and my daughter, I knew that he understood the realities of this situation far better than I. I knew that I had the grace of God, and I wondered what strength he drew on to tell me what he had just said. While he was still within earshot, I choked out the words, "I'm praying for you, too."

He turned around and there was contact—no statement, yet understanding. He nodded. *Is that love I see in his eyes? Certainly compassion.* I believed he was thanking me for understanding his dilemma.

My few months in the pastorate had given me a confidence around hospitals. I knew that a brief and respectful inquiry would not hinder the workers in the ICU if I waited until they looked up from their work to acknowledge me. "I'm John Vaughn. When can I see my wife and daughter?" I asked. The nurse laid aside her clipboard and drew me to one side. "Mr. Vaughn, some of us here know who you are; some of us are Christians, and we're praying. Your wife is in this room here, and Becky is next to her."

I was separated from the two of them by a thick glass window. The little rooms were so small. The doors were closed. Before I could ask why no one was with them, she showed me a bank of monitors at the nurses' station. "We're monitoring their vital signs from these stations. It's best they get some rest and stay as quiet as possible. You can come in and ask questions whenever you like." As though offering me privileged information, she stated, "If you'll be quiet and remain out of the way, I don't think anyone will mind if you stay here by the window. But we can only allow you in their room for five minutes every two hours." She then added, "Mr. Vaughn, they wouldn't know you were there anyway."

She was right. I peered into the two sterile rooms cluttered with medical equipment. I knew it was Brenda and Becky, but they were so far from me. I couldn't touch them or speak to them. All I could do was pray. *All right then, that's what I will do.* For a very long time, I stared at the monitors as my prayer became a wishful recitation. *One more beat, one more, one more.*

A phone rang. *Oh, no! I've got to call the family.*

I briefly glanced once more into the rooms where Brenda and Becky lay asleep. Then I pushed open the double doors of the ICU and walked down the hall. I found a phone booth and called my parents first. It was nearly midnight. Just three hours since the accident. It had seemed like days. Mom answered the phone.

"Is Dad there?" I asked.

"What's wrong, Honey?"

"I just need to talk to Dad."

"Honey, what's the matter?" she pressed.

"Mom, just let me talk to Dad." Mom was so tenderhearted. I knew I couldn't tell her myself. Dad would have to do it.

Dad was on the phone in an instant. "What's the matter, buddy?"

"We had a fire, Dad. Brenda and Becky are hurt real bad. I'm at the Greenville General Hospital."

"Do you want us to come?" he asked.

I couldn't answer. *What is this feeling?* It wasn't the grief to which I had become numb in the last couple of hours. It wasn't sorrow. And then I knew: It was the old anger and shame! *I don't want him to be strong, I thought. I want to be the strong one.* I wanted to show Dad that I could take this like a man.

"God," I prayed, "I'm almost thirty years old. When is this going to end?"

Just tell him, I ordered myself. I couldn't tell if I was angry at Dad for making me feel so dependent, or angry at myself for knowing that if I tried to talk again, I would probably choke up.

Finally, I said what I really wanted to say. "Yeah."

"We're on our way," he said, then hung up.

I needed to call Brenda's dad and stepmother. All the numbers I needed were written in my pocket calendar. I was glad I had them. I took out a clean, white handkerchief from my hip pocket. I always carried one, sometimes two. *Thanks for the sinus problem too, Dad,* I thought to myself. *All the men in our family have it. I wonder if he needs directions? No, Dad doesn't need directions to any place he decides to go; he'll be fine.*

I asked the operator to bill the call to my home phone. "Will someone be home to verify the number?" the operator asked. "Uh, no," I paused, "we had a fire," I started to explain.

Maybe I should witness to her too, I thought, but Bill had answered the phone by then.

"Dad."

"Yes, John, what's the matter?" He knew that something was wrong. They always went to bed early, and we never called them late at night. I told Bill that Brenda and Becky had both been burned and were in intensive care. He was reassuring. He had complete confidence in me. He said, "I'm glad you're with them."

"I think you should try to come," I said. "Both of them are in critical condition. Becky probably won't make it."

"John, we'll be there in five hours."

Leaving from Corbin, Kentucky, as soon as possible, they would have to drive until dawn on Sunday morning just to get to the hospital. I was glad they were coming.

No sense in waking the others up, I thought. *I'll call them in the morning.*

Chapter Five

So then death worketh in us, but life in you.
2 Corinthians 4:12

SUNDAY, 3:00 A.M.

The intensive care waiting room was filled with cigarette smoke. Al brought me some food. Kelly had returned with the shaving kit. *Mom and Dad will be here any minute.*

As I pointed a thumb at the ICU doors to indicate I was going back in, Al looked at me sleepily. He would tell Mom and Dad where I was when they arrived. I was hypnotized again by the monitors when I felt Dad's arm around my shoulder. There was that feeling again. I wanted him there, but I resented his knowing it. We walked over to look through the windows where Brenda and Becky lay. I was exhausted from being up all night, and I was unsure what lay ahead. Certainly, I was in no shape to try to cope with the lingering turmoil in the relationship between my father and me. But the thoughts and the tension were there, and I couldn't make them go away. *Why is it still so difficult for us?*

Pain bridges the "generation gap," a term popularized when I was a teen. Like every generation, my generation thought it was the first one ever to be misunderstood by (or to misunderstand) their parents.

43

We were the "baby boomers." We had a name, and we named all our problems. Dad was a teen in the depression. He learned the hard realities of life. He didn't say "I love you," but he showed it. He was there. There was food on the table. He went to work every day. We had what we needed.

But my generation had to talk it out, drive it into the ground, analyze, and reanalyze, until the problem being discussed got so complicated there was no hope of making a simple statement to clear it up.

We stood there in the Intensive Care Unit, Dad's arm around me and mine around him. I suppose every young man who has ever grown up and had kids of his own sooner or later comes to realize, that sons see themselves as the men they are becoming, and dads see their sons as the boys they used to be. At the time, I thought I was strong, drawing on my spirituality, but I was really drawing strength from Dad.

I had decided a couple of years after my salvation that I was going to make things right with Dad, but I didn't know then just how long it would actually take. I still wouldn't know for years to come the heartache I had caused him. But now he stood beside me as my wife and daughter lay dying. *I sure get myself in a lot of messes,* I thought. *Dad laid it on me pretty heavy in past years, but he was always there.* I couldn't possibly know that night that the pain in a father's heart when a living son does wrong hurts like a father's pain when he sees his child near death.

We went back to the waiting room. As briefly and clearly as I could, I explained what had happened. "The gas can, there in the utility room—somehow Becky had gotten it open. I suppose the heat from the oven ignited it." In spite of the horror of the event, neither at that moment nor after was there a hint of blame or recrimination from anyone.

There I stood, a young Baptist preacher, and there was my dad, a veteran of nearly thirty years in the ministry. He too was a preacher, but Dad was a Methodist. Our differences wore theological garb. But that night, we both understood that God was in control.

Dad had brought with him an old Bible that was very special. In 1957 Dad had been in a terrifying accident. One morning on his way to the school where he taught high-school English, he had been forced off the road by a reckless driver. The big, black 1953 Buick was heavy, and Dad had lost control, slid down a steep bank and into a river. He had never learned to swim, and he narrowly escaped with his life. Later that day he watched helplessly as the car was dragged out of the water. Hoping to salvage his briefcase and papers, Dad waited anxiously as the water drained out of the car. He opened the door and a muddy torrent poured out onto his feet. Dad noticed his Bible lying open on the seat. The first thing he saw was a verse he had underlined in college. "When thou passest through the waters, I will be with thee; and through the rivers, they shall not overflow thee" (Isa. 43:2a).

That night in the hospital, Dad handed me the old Bible without comment and pointed to the second half of the verse. "When thou walkest through the fire, thou shalt not be burned; neither shall the flame kindle upon thee."

We made small talk. We drank coffee. We waited, and I watched the monitor when I could. At dawn, Brenda's folks came, and I related the story to them. Then Bill and Brenda's step-mother, Ollie, kept company with Mom and Dad as I kept my vigil and prayed my repetitious prayer while watching the faint signal on Becky's heart monitor. The morning wore on. I dozed in and out of sleep.

* * *

I forced my eyes open, and my father was there. Dad has always been a very tenderhearted, sentimental man. How hard this must be for him. I have to say something . . . anything to make him feel better.

"Daddy, I look like something they dragged up out of the swamp."

Bless his heart. With tears in his eyes, he looked at me and smiled. "Honey, I've seen you look worse than this when you get up in the morning."

I know now that he must have stumbled out of that room and wept because his heart was broken for me.

* * *

Brenda was heavily sedated. During one of my brief, five-minute visits, I was sure she had heard me, but she had, in fact, only groaned. Becky was completely unconscious. In the late morning, two dear friends, my dentist and a co-worker from one of my previous jobs, came to see me. Pastor Handford had reported the fire to his congregation and there had been a special time of prayer there at his church. Dr. Clark and Brad had left the service to come and be with me. Both of these men would come to help me at Faith Baptist. Both were to be deacons. Both are still dear friends.

The hospital shift had changed. There were now new nurses and new doctors, but everyone seemed to know all about Brenda and Becky. They seemed to know who I was. They were so helpful.

Sometime that morning I called my brother, Harold. He and Linda had a daughter named Angela five days older than Becky. Harold and I had grown even closer as adults than we had been when growing up. We were only twenty months apart and had done practically everything together, but now we enjoyed a new camaraderie. He was very reassuring to me. Then I called our sister, Nancy. Her tender heart made it difficult for both of us, but as always, she encouraged me and gave me strength. I also called my aunt and my grandmother in Kentucky. They started a prayer chain that circled the globe in the days ahead. They had always prayed for me.

The next few hours were a blur. I was exhausted, and things were happening so fast. Shortly before noon, a doctor came to tell me, "We're going to transfer your wife and daughter to another hospital. We've made arrangements for them to go to the Medical University of South Carolina in Charleston. They have a very good burn unit there, and they should be able to take care of them much better than we can. I think they are stable enough to make the trip. We're making transportation arrangements." He then hurried away.

Within an hour, someone came back to let me know a helicopter was on its way from Fort Jackson in Columbia, South Carolina. It would evidently land on top of the hospital. I was told that Brenda was conscious and that I could go in and see her. I rushed to her bedside to learn that they had already explained the transfer to her.

"How's Becky?" she asked.

"Honey, I don't know. She's hurt really bad. They are doing all they can."

We had to make decisions fast. The nurses were preparing Brenda for the trip and obviously waiting for me to leave the room.

"I'll secure the house and drive down with the kids tomorrow. I'll be there as soon as I can," I said.

I still couldn't touch her or kiss her, but we prayed together. The wait had been tedious, and now everything was happening so quickly.

* * *

Late Sunday morning I was aware of John and the doctor near my bed. "I'm going to give her a haircut," the doctor said.

Will he make it look good? I wondered. It's a good thing I could not see what I looked like. The doctor began cutting off all the charred, scorched parts of my hair.

"We're going to send you and Becky to Charleston in a helicopter," he told me. "The facilities are much better there."

I had never flown in a helicopter before, and I was afraid I would get airsick. I tend to get motion sickness even in the car. When I was a child, my father preached in a lot of little churches that were thirty miles or more from home over curvy mountain roads. I think I arrived at church almost every Sunday morning carsick, hanging my head out the window trying to get fresh air. *How will I handle a helicopter ride?*

* * *

I briefly explained to the family that we would all need to be supportive of each other for quite some time. The nurse then told us that Brenda and Becky were already gone. I got the name and address of the hospital and the phone numbers of the contacts I would need to make in that area.

Someone asked me, "Where will you spend the night?"

"I don't know," I answered. "I guess I'll get a motel room." I hadn't even thought much about my own church services that morning. I had previously scheduled a missionary to preach, so the preaching services were covered.

As we were walking down the hall to leave the hospital, our dear friend, Mrs. Smith, came toward me, a spring in her step that belied her seventy-five years. She had always been ready to help us out. "You have no TV at all?" she had asked one time when I told her why we couldn't watch the 1976 Republican Convention. I didn't tell her that we had gotten rid of it deliberately; so, later that day, she had driven up with a brand-new, black-and-white Magnavox portable. She knocked over the mailbox when she pulled into the driveway making the delivery, and she insisted on paying for that, too. We had asked her in for fellowship one time, and she noticed that Debbie needed a bed; she had been sleeping on a little cot. A few days later the call came, "Would you folks be able to use a bed that I don't need anymore? I need to get rid of it, and I'd like for you folks to have it." It was a beautiful, expensive mahogany bed she had obviously bought just for us.

Mrs. Smith could see we were leaving. "I'm not going to keep you," she said, "but you're going to need this, so you take it." She handed me a check for fifty dollars.

* * *

I shouldn't have worried about the helicopter ride. I was asleep most of the time and hardly realized what was going on. I had only one waking moment in the helicopter. Becky and I lay in stretchers suspended like bunk beds. She was above me. I couldn't see her, but I could see the bottom of the stretcher.

Should I speak to her? If she hears me and can't get to me, it might upset her. I had been told that Becky probably would not live. *This might be the last chance I'll ever have to speak to her. I want to tell her that I love her—just one last time. But if I upset her, it might make her physical situation worse.* So I kept quiet. Later I found out that she was unconscious and would not have heard me anyway.

When we arrived in Charleston, we landed on the rooftop of the hospital. Medical personnel converged on us and rushed us inside. Dimly I realized that they were taking Becky in a different direction from me. I did not realize it would be many months before I would see my little girl again. They took me to the Hubbard tank room. "Tank room" is a phrase that strikes fear in the heart of every burn patient. Those who have been there never want to go back. There is a big, steel, oblong tub filled with an antiseptic solution. A stretcher and hoist with chains lowers the patient into the tub. To me, it looked like a torture chamber! I was placed on the stretcher, swung over the tank, and half submerged. Two doctors and two nurses scrubbed me from head to toe with rolls of gauze. Open flesh being scrubbed and rinsed in such an immodest environment is painful and embarrassing. Some patients have broken their own teeth from the pain of debridement in the tank room. Twice a day I faced this humiliation. I was raised out of the tank and wrapped in sterile gauze with ointment liberally spread over my body.

"So this is debridement," I declared. *How will Becky ever survive this horrible treatment? How will I?*

* * *

Though Bill, Brenda's dad, was a part-time Baptist preacher, he and Ollie both had regular, weekday jobs and had to get back for work on Monday morning. My mother taught school, and there were a few days of school left, but she could call a substitute teacher for her second-grade class. Dad knew his ministry was with me, at least for another day or so. He left to reserve a couple of motel rooms not far from our house. I learned that a family from our church had gone out late Saturday night to get Debbie and Johnny and take them to their home. They had children about the same ages. I picked Debbie and Johnny up and explained the events of the night before.

We ate and then spent that Sunday night together in the motel. Before turning the lights off, I called the hospital in Charleston. The nurses were very reassuring. Brenda was on the fifth floor in the burn unit, Becky on the ninth floor in Pediatric Intensive Care. I gave them my number and asked them to call me if there was any change. For a brief moment, the children were able to talk to Mommy on the phone. Her voice sounded strong. A wave of hope swept over me as I heard her voice, so familiar, so reassuring. I couldn't see her wounds or smell what would become the sickeningly familiar smell of the burn unit. The children and I prayed, committing Mommy and Becky to the Lord. We were all asleep in less than a minute.

* * *

The first night in Charleston, the doctors didn't tell me very much. *Why don't they talk to me? Why don't they tell me what's going on?* I felt very much alone. John was coming, of course, as soon as he could make arrangements. But he didn't have the benefit of a helicopter ride. I was scared and in a lot of pain. I could hear the doctors complaining, sometimes even cursing, because they could not get a permanent IV line put into my arms. There was simply no place to put it. Everything was raw and bleeding. *They're angry with me. What am I doing wrong? I can't do anything!*

Later I realized that they were not angry with me, but with the situation. I was in critical condition, and they were fighting to save my life. It seemed to them that I might not make it. Finally, they put in a subclavian IV—a direct line surgically placed below the collarbone. This lifeline would remain in place for months.

Being in intensive care was an unsettling situation. Through the curtains, I could hear people in the beds next to me. Their groans of pain never stopped, even during sleep. And I, too, was doing my share.

Jennifer was my nurse. She would become a personal friend in the days ahead. Later we laughed about my telling her my feet were stuck to the bed. I don't know how many times I pleaded, "Please help me, my feet are stuck." It must have been a feeling of heaviness from the medication, or perhaps the weight of the cooling blanket that caused me to feel I could not move my feet.

Time after time she patiently responded, "Your feet are fine, Brenda. They're not stuck."

A resident whom we called Dr. Ray—that may have been his first name—cared for me that first night. The Medical University of South Carolina is a teaching hospital. Interns and nurses rotate in and out constantly. Dr. Ray was affectionately dubbed "the burn unit marshmallow," although he tried to appear very gruff.

During the following days I often became angry with Dr. Ray on trips to the tank room because he insisted I move from my bed to a stretcher by myself. Moving at all was excruciatingly painful for me. He would order, "Move! Now!"

"I can't! I can't move!"

"Yes, you can," he would insist, allowing no one to help me.

I know now that he persisted for my own good. I had to keep my joints flexible. Dr. Ray kept this gruff demeanor to control his genuine compassion. He didn't want to become emotional in front of his patients.

The burn unit was traumatic even for the medical personnel. The turnover of full-time personnel is great because the stress is almost unbearable. It is impossible to help a burned patient without causing terrible pain. Many people, even professionals, simply cannot tolerate that kind of stress.

The stress for the patient is almost as hard to bear as the pain. Beyond the physical injuries, mental anguish and fear affect recovery and can bring death. That night, in spite of the powerful medication, I began to realize the intensity of the unending pain that would remain with me for many months.

I determined to wait patiently for John to arrive. Oh, how I wished he would come quickly! I tried to focus my mind on other things. I wondered if anyone had called my mother. What would happen if my mother, father, and stepmother were all together in this room? How will John handle that? The emotional climate of troubled relationships in my family was always uncertain. My last conscious thought that night was, *Lord, give us wisdom.*

Chapter Six

We having the same spirit of faith . . . we also believe, and therefore speak; knowing that he which raised up the Lord Jesus shall raise up us also by Jesus . . .

2 Corinthians 4:13–14

MONDAY, 10:30 A.M.

Late in the morning the ringing phone awoke me. *That's news of Brenda,* I thought. Dad looked in from the adjoining motel room. "Someone from the insurance company has been calling," he said.

I had only three suits and was wearing one of them on the night of the fire. The other two and some of my other clothes had been taken to the laundry early Monday morning. The children's clothes had been gathered up and laundered by the ladies in the church. The clothes were there for us when we woke up late Monday morning. I let the children watch TV while I showered and dressed.

* * *

It was frustrating not to be able to see Becky, not to be able to comfort her, not to be able to give her a mother's love. I was in serious trouble myself, drifting in and out of consciousness and only half aware of what was going

52

on. I was so involved in my own fear and my own pain that I was not as aware of her situation as John was.

Will she live? How will I stand it if she doesn't? I felt that I knew better than anyone the kind of pain she was suffering, but her burns were actually worse than mine. She was too little even to have the comfort of understanding why she had pain. Oh, Lord, she must be so afraid! Would it be better if she died? She could come home to be with you. She might have brain damage—she'll be handicapped! Lord, maybe You should just take her and give me the strength to bear it.

But then I would remember her as she used to be and how much I enjoyed her. Then I would beg God to leave her—I would be willing to take whatever He gave us, to be able to enjoy having her for a few more years. This battle raged in my mind until I realized that here too was a lesson the Lord had for me: it wasn't my decision to make. With that knowledge came true comfort. *Lord, You do what's best, and then give me the grace to accept whatever it is and to make a blessing out of it.*

That prayer didn't come the first day or the first week. It was a sorting-through process that took time in the torment of emotional and physical pain. God never told me I couldn't cry, or that I had to be perfect, or that I had to witness flawlessly to everyone who walked into my room. He knew my heart, and I came to realize that He was asking only that I be faithful—only that I trust Him to do what was best.

In the early days all I could get was partial information about Becky. "She's still alive," the hospital staff told me. "But she's still unconscious."

Oh, Becky! I thought. *Are there any thoughts in your mind right now? Do you remember our games and playtimes?* I used to get Debbie and Johnny off to school and John would leave. I'd give Becky her breakfast, then dress her, and then we'd play. We'd play house, we'd play dolls, we'd play on the bed at nap time, telling stories and giggling together until she would fall asleep. *What a precious child she's been to me!*

Now I could only lie in that bed and wonder about Becky. *Can she feel the pain? Is she scared? Is she lonely? Oh, Lord, can I really stand it if You take her home? What has she done in her small life to deserve this?* I knew that God had every reason to punish me, but I couldn't imagine Him wanting to punish a two-year-old child. *Is He punishing her because I have been unfaithful? Oh, I hope not!* My fear for Becky's life brought back some of the feelings I'd known when my only brother died. I had been just fourteen. My parents had grieved and been driven further apart by the senseless loss of their only son to a drunken driver's folly. I had been angry at them for years for not responding better to that tragedy, but now I tasted the anguish they must have felt.

* * *

MONDAY, 12:00 NOON

████████████████████████████████ I was cleaned up and dressed, and we were trying to decide what to do. I didn't know how much needed to be done before we left for Charleston, but I knew I needed to make some long-range plans for the ministry, covering all the services until I could get back. Of course, I'd have to secure the house somehow. Mom and Dad were still with me. The insurance people had called again while I was cleaning up. There was a number where I was to return the call.

That Monday afternoon, the stress was beginning to take its toll. God had us in a pressure cooker. The "smelting process" had begun. Before the dross could be burned away, it would have to rise to the top—and some of the things that would come to the surface would not be pleasant. As the stress increased and our sense of helplessness set in, our reactions turned into overreactions. Dad and I assumed the other's wrong responses were based on wrong beliefs.

We exchanged angry words. He must have known the trouble was more than just the pressure of the family's injuries. I still felt that I had something to prove. This was my opportunity to show Dad that my church was better than his, and that, therefore, my worth as a person demanded his respect. If I could show him that I had what it took to deal with a crisis like this, once and for all the old father/son rivalry would come to an end, and I would be the winner. I had not yet come to realize that we never establish our own value as persons in the eyes of others by demeaning their value. A son cannot earn his father's respect with disrespect.

More important than all of these things was something yet unknown to me. God had something to prove to me—that my struggle was not unique. Along with the many lessons we would learn in the days ahead, there would be one that every young man must come to learn in the rite of passage into manhood and mutual friendship with his father. When children hurt, fathers hurt in a way those children cannot know. I would come to see that my own struggle to find my place in life would become less and less important as I entered more and more into the struggle of my child. Maybe that's what being a parent is all about. I was going to realize an important principle that has since become a cornerstone in my ministry to families: God does not give us children because we have the ability to raise them; He gives us children so we can learn from them how to help them raise theirs.

Mom and Dad left after the argument. He knew what I didn't at that time, but there was nothing he could say or do to help me through what lay ahead.

I loaded Debbie and Johnny into the car and drove to the house to make it as secure as possible. It was midafternoon, but the house looked unusually dark. The power was off, and the walls were blackened with soot. I was surprised at how little structural damage there was—how normal everything looked from the outside. We were supposed to transfer possession of the house to the new owners in less than two weeks. There would be no way now that we could meet that deadline. I was sure they would understand. The front door was locked, and the windows were closed. The large picture window in the living room was framed with the melted remains of the shades and drapes. The back door where Brenda had escaped with Becky was badly burned. Charred remains of appliances and kitchen utensils were strewn around the yard, left there by the firemen who had saved the rest of the house from destruction. Someone had nailed a board over the doorway. It wasn't secure, but it was an effort. I had no tools to make it stronger so I hoped it would be enough.

We stopped at a discount store, and I let the children pick out two toys each. They would need something to do in the days ahead. We stopped for hamburgers, and while the children ate, I made a list of all the people I needed to contact. The deacons would take care of the church. I would need to cash the $50 check from Mrs. Smith. We had just over $6,000 in our savings account from the sale of the house, and we had put $150 earnest money down on a new house closer to the church. I would need to call the seller. It would be better to lose the earnest money than to spend the savings on a house I might not need. If Brenda and Becky didn't make it, our future was very uncertain. Debbie and Johnny played quietly in the car with their toys while I made the calls.

Of course, the deacons would take care of anything that happened at church. My supervisor at United Parcel Service was also helpful. "Take all the time you need," he said. "We've checked your insurance. Your wife and daughter are covered."

This was unbelievable! From a fifteen-hour-a-week, part-time job, UPS would cover nearly $200,000 in medical expenses in the months ahead. I couldn't reach the man from whom we were buying the house. Someone from church would call him in the next few days. Not only would he let us out of the deal, but he would send the earnest money back. There would be hundreds of acts of generosity like these in the days ahead. Without them, we couldn't have survived. The small church was paying me just $45 a week, and I was making another $90 from the part-time work I had started again a month before at United Parcel Service. The brief figures I had compiled on the back of a napkin gave me no clue to God's plan for the marvelous provision of tens of thousands of dollars.

It was nearly eight o'clock when we pulled out of Greenville and headed southeast down the interstate. The kids fell asleep, and the kaleidoscope of memories began. I was trying to make sense of it all: the conflict with Dad, yet the compassion that I had felt from him; the long night in the ICU; and the Army helicopter chopping its way to Charleston ahead of me the day before. I relived that endless night in the ICU, and then all I could see was the heart monitor. It loomed large and filled my field of vision. I could almost hear the heartbeat . . . steady now, rhythmic . . . faster . . . faster. The green glow of the screen blurred before me, but it wasn't the heartbeat I heard, it was the sound of my tires on the seams in the road. And it wasn't the monitor I saw, but the sign for the first Charleston exit. I had arrived!

Chapter Seven

For all things are for your sakes, that the abundant grace might through the thanksgiving of many redound to the glory of God. For which cause we faint not; but though our outward man perish, yet the inward man is renewed day by day.

2 Corinthians 4:15–16

MONDAY, 11:05 P.M.

The gas gauge was below empty—for how long, I had no idea. Ironic that a gallon of gas had caused this problem, and now I was wondering if I would run out before I could find a filling station. I did not want to get off at an unfamiliar exit, and then the exit for the Charleston Air Force Base caught my eye. I saw a sign indicating a station was open. In what was to be one of thousands of providential meetings, the Lord led me not just to a particular place, but to a particular person.

I coasted up the exit ramp, turned back across the interstate, and down the hill to River Road. I turned into the station and pulled alongside the pump. Debbie and Johnny were still asleep in the back seat. I put twenty-four gallons in the twenty-four-gallon tank, checked the oil, cleaned the windshield, and went inside to pay. The attendant was reading the Bible.

"You a Christian?" I asked, somewhat surprised.

He looked up with a smile. "As a matter of fact, I just became a Christian," he beamed.

"That's great. Have you found a good Bible-believing church yet?" I asked, as I handed him the cash for my gasoline.

"Well, I've been going to a little church over here on the other side of River Road. The pastor is good, and he really teaches the Bible." He was counting out my change.

"Well, that's the most important thing," I retorted. "I'm a preacher myself." Another customer came in, but I asked briefly before I left, "Can you tell me how to find the Medical University Hospital?"

"Sure," the attendant replied as he reached for a Charleston map. He was a conscientious man. While he helped the other customer, he instructed me how to find the area I needed on the map. When he was finished with the customer, he took a pen and marked the route I needed to take, circled the location of the hospital, then inquired, "Do you have a family member in the hospital?"

"Yes," I told him, "we had a fire on Saturday night. My wife and daughter were badly burned." He listened with genuine interest as I told him what had happened.

Then he said, "Look, there's a verse here I was reading a while ago. It's in Romans. 'And we know that all things work together for good to them that love God, to them who are the called according to his purpose.' Romans 8:28."

"That's a tremendous promise," I replied.

"Hey, listen," the man said, "why don't we pray before you go?" He then lifted up his voice in the sweet and simple phrases of genuine trust so characteristic of a new Christian. We smiled and shook hands, and I was on my way. I never saw the man again, though I stopped at that station to look for him on other trips. In the months ahead, God was going to ask me for thousands of spontaneous testimonies about the Lord, but for now He was firmly assuring me of His presence and the prayers of others for my family.

It was nearly midnight by the time I worked my way through the city of Charleston, found the hospital complex, and then located the right building. I had awakened the children while looking for a parking place. We were in the hospital and on our way up to the fifth floor when I learned that the children would not be able to go with me. For now I had to leave Debbie and Johnny in the waiting room as I went up to see Brenda on the fifth floor.

I stopped outside the security doors and read a sign instructing me to put on a surgical gown, shoe covers, and a surgical cap. I did and passed through the double doors and into a long hallway. Another set of doors was permanently closed at the other end. The first room on the right was a hospital room converted into a lounge where I would be invited to relax many times in the months ahead. To the left was a darkened room with a sign above it bearing the simple words, "Hubbard Tank." Three or four rooms lined each side of the hall, then at the far end on the left was a nurses' station and what was apparently the intensive care ward within the burn unit itself. A pungent, medicinal smell saturated the air. I would later learn it was an ointment called Silvadene, used liberally on every patient at every dressing change.

The burn unit was not in a typical hospital. This was a medical university with tired interns and nurses who attended classes in addition to working their shifts. But there was an intensity of commitment here—a sense of urgency and dedication. *Brenda will be safe here*, I thought.

The doctors and nurses were expecting me. A young nurse stepped out of the intensive care unit and walked toward me.

"You must be Reverend Vaughn," she said softly.

"Yes, ma'am."

"Let's sit here and talk for just a moment before you go in to see your wife," she said.

We sat down on the overstuffed vinyl chairs placed along the sides of the hallway. "Your wife is awake, and she's been expecting you. I want to tell you what you're going to see and also ask you not to stay very long. There's another patient in intensive care, a teenage boy who probably is not going to make it. He is behind the curtain on the other side of the room. You won't see him, but there will be some activity over there. Don't let this bother you." She looked to see what my reaction would be.

"No problem," I said.

"Brenda is getting some strong pain medication, so she is not going to be very alert. She may drift in and out as you talk to her. Her vital signs are good. She's breathing well and taking fluids. The doctor can explain all of this to you tomorrow, and there will be some paperwork you'll need to take care of downstairs. There are just a couple of things you need to know for tonight."

"Okay, fine," I replied.

"When someone has been burned as badly as your wife, the first thing we do is to perform an escarotomy on each arm and leg. That's a procedure in which an incision is made through all three layers of burned skin. The underlying tissues swell; otherwise circulation could be cut off. Brenda has had escarotomies on both arms and legs." As I waited for more information, she added, "Reverend Vaughn, this is not very pleasant to look at and, frankly, when we're trying to help someone survive, we can't be too concerned with modesty."

"I understand," I said.

"Okay, let's go say 'Hi' to Brenda." I don't remember hesitating or being weak, but I do remember the nurse leading me by the arm down the hallway and into the Intensive Care Unit. I surveyed the room for an instant to familiarize myself. There was a doctor with a clipboard signing papers. A couple of nurses were talking behind the curtain where the young man lay dying, and another nurse was standing at the foot of the other bed, blocking my view. As we walked in, she stepped aside.

I looked at Brenda, and my knees began to buckle. *How can she even be alive, let alone conscious?* When I last saw her, she was all soot and gauze, but here lay a mass of raw, bleeding flesh! I stepped up beside the bed and called her softly, "Honey." I absolutely would not have recognized her if I had not been told it was her. Her eyes blinked open; she smiled. No question about it, it was Brenda; nothing had changed but our circumstances.

"I look like something that crawled out of a swamp," she joked.

"You have looked better," I affirmed. "How do you feel?"

"Believe it or not," she said, "I feel better." She rolled her eyes sleepily. "I could really get used to this Demerol."

What a woman, I thought. *I came here to comfort her, and she's comforting me.*

"Where are the kids?" she asked.

"Downstairs in the waiting room. I can't stay long. They're really tired. We're going to stay at Charlie's. It's back about fifteen or twenty miles the way we came." A former neighbor of ours named Charlie had moved from Greenville to Charleston. A mutual friend had called him, and he was expecting us whenever we arrived that night.

"You go on," she directed. "Get some rest. They really know what they're doing here. I'll be fine."

"I love you," I told her.

"I love you, too."

I swallowed hard, hoping she wouldn't ask, but then she did, choking back the tears. "How's Becky? Is she still alive?"

"I don't know, Honey. I haven't been up to see her yet. They told me she's on the ninth floor in Pediatric Intensive Care. I'm going to see her now. I'll stop by and let you know on my way out." She closed her eyes tightly and nodded her head.

Back through the double doors, I deposited the surgical clothes in a hamper and searched for the elevator. It would be awhile before I would learn the shortcuts, and the visitor elevators seemed to take forever.

The Pediatric Intensive Care Unit was really just a large room at the end of a hallway. It was in a new wing of the hospital and smelled fresh and clean. It was obviously not a burn unit. The door was open, and the light was on over the nurse's desk. A little boy with his head heavily bandaged lay in a small bed. Partially hidden behind a curtain was a stainless steel crib with the sides down. Next to it was a heart monitor, an IV, and a respirator. A nurse was standing beside the bed. Becky's little form lay there almost lifeless. I had steel taps on my heels to keep them from wearing out, and I had to tiptoe to keep them quiet. The nurse must have known I was Becky's father, because she motioned for me to come and stand beside the bed. The heavy bandages were gone. Now there were light gauze bandages smeared with the white Silvadene ointment. Large gaping incisions told me the doctors had also performed an escarotomy on both arms and legs, and on each side of Becky's torso. The wounds gaped and bled as her chest expanded with the rhythm of the respirator. Most shocking of all, her eyes were still open! Her eyelids had been burned so severely, and the tissue beneath was so swollen, that the eyelids were turned inside out. Her mouth was open and the lips pulled back away from the teeth. Her hair was gone—washed away with the other soot and ashes. Like Brenda, she had a subclavian IV, a small tube inserted directly into a vein beneath her collarbone.

I looked at her hands—those sweet little hands I'd held in my own, those little hands that would play for hours, making a game of even the simplest things. Becky would sit quietly at the table waiting for the meal to begin. One day she had turned her spoon over and covered it with her napkin like a blanket. She had patted the spoon lovingly with those little hands, kissed it and said, "Night-night spoon," then looked up at me with a smile.

I reached out to touch her hand. The fingers were as black as charcoal. They were hard. Ceramic. *I wonder if she will lose her fingers?* Finally, I asked the nurse, "How is she?"

Her answers were technical and informative, and they offered no hope of Becky's survival. "She's on 100 percent oxygen. We're giving her some nourishment and trying to keep her body fluids in balance. There hasn't been much change."

"So, what do you think?" I asked.

She looked at me sympathetically, patted my shoulder, turned and walked away. I told Becky I loved her. I prayed with her and knew that there was nothing I could do. As I turned to leave the room, I again noticed the little boy with the big gauze turban on his head.

"Excuse me, nurse, what's this little boy's trouble?"

"The Lane boy?" she asked, surprised that I wanted to know. "He is hydro-encephalic," she said. "He had a shunt put in. The other day he had a serious infection."

I stood at the foot of his bed for a few moments and thought of Johnny. This little boy was not much older than Johnny had been when he had had surgery on his head. *Oh, if only we had been living for the Lord then,* I thought. *I wonder what source of strength this family has.* I prayed there for the little fellow and his family and went back down to say goodnight to Brenda. It took longer to get into the scrub clothes than to give Brenda the brief report that Becky was unconscious and doing about the same.

Brenda was relieved that Becky was alive and not aware of what was going on, but she cried, "I can't do anything for her. I can't do anything to help her!—Tell Debbie and Johnny I love them."

"You just concentrate on getting well," I stated. "We'll be just fine. Everybody is doing everything possible to help us." I prayed with her briefly, then said, "We'll see you in the morning."

Debbie and Johnny were still awake. There was a TV on in the visitors' lounge, and they were waiting patiently. "I'm so proud of you both," I encouraged them. "You're being so sweet."

"How's Mommy?" Debbie inquired cautiously.

"Well, Honey, Mommy has been hurt real bad, and it's going to be a long time before she's able to come home again; but this is a nice hospital, and they're taking good care of her. She wants you both to know she loves you very much and she's sorry she can't be with you."

"How's Becky?" Johnny asked quietly.

"Becky's sleeping," I reassured them. "The Lord will take care of them both. We need to go now and find the place we're going to stay."

Chapter Eight

For our light affliction, which is but for a moment, worketh for us a far more exceeding and eternal weight of glory.

2 Corinthians 4:17

TUESDAY, 1:00 A.M.

It was after one o'clock. Charlie answered the phone with a sleepy voice. "John?"

"Where can I meet you?" I asked.

He gave me directions to a shopping center near his home, right off the interstate. We were there in twenty minutes. Charlie was standing beside his car in the empty parking lot. I pulled up beside him. When I got out, he threw his arms around me and hugged me for a long time. Holding me by the shoulders, he said, "I love you just that much. How are you doing?"

"I'll make it," I declared. "The Lord is helping us tremendously. Right now, I think we better get the kids to bed."

"Sure, no problem," he said.

We followed him to his house. Jeanette had rearranged her own three children so that Debbie would sleep in a room with her daughter, and Johnny in the other room with the boys. Charlie and Jeanette had already explained to their kids that they should get up quietly in the morning and let my children sleep. The house was not large and the furnishings were modest, but they had made arrangements for me to have a room to myself. Debbie and Johnny fell asleep right away, but I stayed up to talk to Charlie and Jeanette and explain what I knew so far. Charlie took the time to give me several names and phone numbers of people I could call on for help, some in his area and others down near the hospital. They had friends in their church who had made their home available for any of our relatives who might want to come visit Brenda and Becky.

The next morning, my kids enjoyed playing in the yard. Since only five days of school was left in Greenville anyway, I had no problem making arrangements for them to be excused. The first full day at the hospital went by quickly. There were dozens of forms to fill out and phone calls to make. I spent at least a full hour changing clothes to go in and out of the burn unit. I met several other patients there. I learned that all were on a first-name basis—patients, nurses, and doctors. It didn't take long to get acquainted; and as the days wore on, there was no need for formality.

Later that week, Brenda's father and stepmother drove down again from Kentucky. They stayed with Charlie's friends and gave me some much-needed companionship in the long hours of waiting in the visitors' lounge. My sister, Nancy, was still living in Myrtle Beach where her fiance—an Air Force officer—was now stationed. She too came for a visit and helped me with the children.

Debbie and Johnny spent their days playing with Charlie and Jeanette's children. I came home one afternoon to find that Johnny had run through the sliding glass door to the patio. Miraculously, the shards of glass had fallen around him, and he was barely scratched. There was no need to bother Brenda with this news. We were thankful to the Lord for His protection of the children, but it was obvious I couldn't care for them properly and spend the necessary time with Brenda and Becky. They would need to be somewhere familiar or with family.

On the fifth day in Charleston, Dr. Otherson, a gentle man who seemed to be in his late fifties, called me in for a meeting. Brenda's folks accompanied me. The doctor explained to us, compassionately but clearly, that Becky was not doing well at all.

"She needs a dimension of care we simply cannot provide," he said. "She's going to have to go to a burn center."

"Do you have any place in mind?" I asked.

"I have contacted five hospitals. The Shriners have three: one in Boston, one in Galveston, and one in Cincinnati. There are also two Army hospitals in Texas." As I waited for more information, he added, "There are no beds available in any of these hospitals, but I could get a call from any of them at any time. I recommend we transfer Becky as soon as a bed comes open, wherever that may be."

Looking in my wallet, I retrieved the card that the deputy had given me in Greenville. "This man told me about the Shriners hospitals. Do you need this?" I asked.

"We are already in touch with the Shriners, of course, but I'll mention his name. If it's all right with you, I'm going to start working on the transportation."

He went on to explain about the care that Becky could get, especially in one of the Shriners hospitals. He was very reassuring about the quality of their care. I wanted desperately to keep Brenda and Becky together, but I knew I had to do what was best for Becky. The criticism some might express if I took help from the Shriners crossed my mind again.

"What do you think, Dad?" I asked.

"John, you're going to have to make this decision yourself," Bill said. "The doctor is giving some good advice."

I looked at the kind doctor and stated my case as plainly as I could. "Of course, I want what's best for both of them. And if this is what Becky needs, then this is what she should have. But doctor, if we know now that Becky's not going to make it, I'd rather keep them together."

"Well," he said, "I can appreciate that, and I would probably want to do the same thing. Frankly, I can't give you much hope for Becky's survival, but she is alive and she has survived for almost a week. As long as she's alive, there is a chance. I think we ought to do everything we can."

"All right, doctor, whatever you think."

Before my sister left, we spent some time with Brenda. I kissed Brenda good-bye, then walked Nancy to her car. She was crying and unable to talk. Although she is six years younger than I, we share a birthday, and we have always been very close. Nancy lived with Brenda for a few months while I was overseas in the Air Force and attended the same college where Brenda and I met.

"It's okay, Nancy. Everything will be all right. God is in control," I said softly as she sobbed.

Finally she managed to say, "No, it's not that . . . I know. . . ."

"It's okay," I said.

"I know," she sobbed. "It's just that . . . seeing you kiss Brenda up there . . . She looks so awful . . . I'm sorry. . . ."

"I understand."

"I'm sorry . . . I know you love her. I love her, too. I guess I never thought any of us would be called to do something like this."

After we said our good-byes, Nancy left. She was to be married in just a few weeks. "For better or worse . . . in sickness and in health" held new meaning for all of us now.

That night, I met the Lanes, the family of the little boy in the PICU. Becky had just returned from surgery to remove some of the burned skin from her torso so she could breathe easier. I was standing by her bedside when the Lanes came in to visit their son. Since he was asleep, they decided not to wake him. We introduced ourselves.

Mrs. Lane then asked, "Is this your little girl?" When I answered, "Yes," she began to cry. Mr. Lane, a tall man, much taller than I, spoke up, "Could we talk to you for just a minute, out here?"

We walked to the waiting area just outside the PICU. The Lanes were both young—mid-twenties, and this was their only child. As we sat down, Mr. Lane explained, "Reverend Vaughn, the nurse told us you prayed for our son. We're both Christians, but we've been out of church ever since our son was born. I guess we've just been mad at God. We haven't been able to understand why He would allow something like this to happen to our baby. But when we saw your daughter, we realized how simple his problem is. When we heard that you had prayed for him, we were ashamed that we haven't trusted the Lord for all these months. Our pastor is no longer at the church we used to attend. We don't know who to call right now. We know we need the Lord's help, but we're not sure what to do."

Their transparency touched my heart. I retrieved my New Testament from my pocket and turned to Romans 8. We talked for over an hour. We prayed together, cried together, and, in that precious bond only Christians know, became friends quickly. Because of surgical complications, their son would be in the hospital for several more days. The three of us met each day for Bible study and prayer. I grew confident they were back on their feet and once again ready to live for the Lord.

The Lanes were staying with an aunt who lived in Charleston. I met her the day after meeting them. She was a sweet, gracious Christian lady who was happy to learn I had talked with the couple the night before. On the eighth day, as I walked to the family room to meet the Lanes for devotions, the receptionist called me with a message. I went to the desk. There I met another member of the Lanes' family. He had bad news, and he asked for my help. Their aunt, who had told him I had been meeting with them, had died of a heart attack shortly after the young couple had left for the hospital that very morning.

"Will you tell them?" he asked me plainly.

Perhaps this was an extreme case, but similar demands have been placed on me again and again in the ministry. This would not be the last time that I would be called upon to lay aside my own grief to comfort others.

The Lanes were shocked, but God confirmed in their hearts the providence of our meeting and how He had prepared them for this news, just as He had wanted to prepare them for the news about their son. This time they were able to respond with the help of God's grace.

A few days later they handed me a small gift. I unwrapped it carefully. It was a copy of Charles M. Sheldon's *In His Steps*. I read it all the way through that night and several more times in the weeks ahead. The little classic offered great comfort to me. I had no idea then how many times I would ask myself, *What would Jesus do?* in the difficult months ahead, especially with Becky needing to be transferred to another hospital.

It was hard to think about leaving Brenda, but we knew Becky needed the best care that she could get. At one point I received what I thought was encouraging news from a young PICU intern. The "news" turned out to be entirely false. The intern told me that new plastic surgery techniques could reduce Becky's scarring to a minimum. "In fact," he said, "she may not even be scarred at all."

Late one evening, a young nurse heard me praying with Becky. I was reassuring her of Jesus' love for her. The nurse interrupted me, "Don't you think it would be better to tell her to trust the doctors and nurses, instead of baby Jesus?"

Baby Jesus? I thought. *What kind of ridiculous comment is that?* I felt the temptation to debate. A sharp rebuke perched on the tip of my tongue when the Lord restrained me. This kind of Christmas-card theology could easily be answered. The woman's comment was completely unprofessional, but she knew I was a preacher. A poor response from me would have offended her far more than she had offended me. *She may have a point. I should be more careful to express my confidence in the doctors and nurses for Becky's sake. She will be completely dependent upon them, especially at another hospital.*

"We'll pray for the Lord to guide the doctors and nurses," I replied.

The same day that I encouraged the Lanes about the unexpected death of their aunt, I received word from Dr. Otherson that one of the hospitals had an opening for Becky. They would transfer her the next day! We had left it completely with the Lord.

Three of the hospitals Dr. Otherson had contacted were in Texas. Because Johnny's surgery had been in a hospital in Texas, and Debbie had been born while I was stationed there, I expected it to be there somehow.

"Cincinnati," he said when I met with him in his office.

"Praise the Lord!" I exclaimed. I then explained that I was from northern Kentucky. "My brother lives very near there. He works in Cincinnati. He has a daughter just five days older than Becky. This will be a tremendous help to our family."

The doctor's staff busily made arrangements for transportation, as I went to share the news with Brenda. I obtained permission to take Debbie and Johnny on the flight with me while I accompanied Becky to the Shriners hospital in Cincinnati. I planned to leave them with my brother, who would arrange for their care. The children would be able to spend time with relatives in Kentucky until we could find out how long Brenda would actually be in the hospital.

I stayed with Brenda late that night. We talked a great deal. Brenda expressed grave concern about her divorced parents seeing one another again after so many years. Her mother was flying in from Ohio, and her father was driving back from Kentucky.

* * *

As I lay in the intensive care section of the burn unit, I worried about the emotional climate should Mom and Dad be at the hospital at the same time. I remembered Mom's frustration at not being able to be present to help me when Johnny was in the hospital. I worried so much about her that her presence brought me more emotional distress than help. I knew bitterness still existed between my mother and my father because of the divorce. I wasn't sure how they were going to react when together, and they would surely be together before my hospitalization was over. I wondered if they would be able to get along well enough to think about my needs.

My stepmother was present too. She is a very sweet lady. I can remember her wiping my brow when I was nauseated. She performed many unpleasant tasks for me. Because I knew what a weak stomach she had, I was filled with love for her as I realized how difficult that must have been. I asked her about it later. "Honey, I asked the Lord to give me the strength to do whatever you needed done," she replied. I marveled at her attitude, yet still felt concern about my parents. I didn't want my stepmother to get caught in the middle.

Of course, God had been working in their lives all these years, as He had in mine. Regardless of how justified we may think it is, the sad truth about bitterness is that it blinds us to the growth in the lives of those against whom we are bitter. My own unresolved anger brought me much fear about whether they were going to get along—whether I was going to have to mediate again.

Mom and Dad were at the hospital together, but they were able to talk about and to deal with some areas where they had both been wrong. It turned out to be a good thing for them—a time of healing, of letting go of the anger they had held toward each other. My mother began to face her bitterness toward my stepmother, and it turned out to be a positive time in all of their lives. Dad later told me, as did Mom, that they had had opportunities in the waiting room to resolve some things. I believe this was the beginning of the healing process between my mother and father.

Gradually, the tension eased, and Mom and Dad became a real comfort to me. My fears diminished. As the days passed, my concern focused more on Becky's inevitable departure.

* * *

MONDAY
MAY 29, 10:00 P.M.

▬▬▬▬▬▬▬▬▬▬▬▬▬▬ Before leaving that night, I stood beside Becky's little bed. She gave no sign of awareness but lay there motionless. I thought about the transfer taking place the next day, whether she would survive the trip, whether Brenda would survive until I returned. The evidence of God's grace in a Christian's life is sometimes hard to understand.

A young nurse on duty that night started talking to me and asking questions about our faith. She wondered about a belief that would enable us to remain strong in a tragedy like this.

"Reverend Vaughn," she asked, "do you want Becky to live, knowing what she has ahead?" It was a sincere question and, frankly, I had not yet asked it of myself.

"Well," I replied, "if you want to know the truth, I would turn the clock back and prevent this thing entirely. But we don't always get what we want in life, so whatever God wants is fine with me."

Chapter Nine

While we look not at the things which are seen, but at the things which are not seen: for the things which are seen are temporal; but the things which are not seen are eternal.

2 Corinthians 4:18

TUESDAY
MAY 30, 8:30 A.M.

The Cessna Citation had flown in from Atlanta the day before. The mechanics had worked on the electrical system so the respiratory therapist traveling with Becky could use the respirator in flight. There was enough room on the plane for a doctor, a nurse, the respiratory therapist, my two older children, and me. They were able to make a little bed for Becky between two seats that faced each other. We were all to be at the airport by 10:00 A.M.

The hospital gave special permission for Debbie and Johnny to visit their mother before we left. It had been eight days since our arrival in Charleston. Brenda had not yet received any skin grafts but the process of debridement was taking place twice a day. She was heavily bandaged, and pigskin grafts covered much of the burned area on her arms and legs. As long as she was not moved too much, the bleeding was minimal.

Since the children could not enter the burn unit, Brenda was brought out to them in a wheelchair. As they wheeled her through the double doors, the bloodstains began to spread on the sheet covering her from her neck down. The children immediately began to cry. It was very hard. Brenda reached toward them, her hands and fingers wrapped thick with blood-stained gauze. The children hesitated, then embraced their mother gently. We all cried. Then we prayed together and said our good-byes.

The children and I left for the airport in the ambulance. I left my car in the parking garage, not knowing for sure when I would return. The sleek little commuter jet was ready. The pilot and copilot took our suitcases. We waited while the doctors and nurses secured Becky in the airplane. The flight from Charleston to Cincinnati took only an hour and fifteen minutes. As we touched down, an ambulance waited on the tarmac at Cincinnati's Lunken Airport. The doctor and nurses went on with Becky in the ambulance, while Debbie, Johnny, and I rode in the Shriners van. By the time we got there, Becky was already in the Intensive Care Unit.

The Shriners Burns Institute brought immediate encouragement to us. The three-story, well-staffed hospital was immaculate. Although it only had fifty beds, it had three times as many employees. An entire floor was committed to research. The patients were housed on the third floor. The east and west units were reverse copies of one another. The central nurses' stations were surrounded by a series of rooms: two large rooms with several beds on one side, three small rooms with individual beds on the other side, and a large Intensive Care Unit immediately across from the nurses' stations. The entire atmosphere communicated one very clear message: This was the best possible place for a burn victim. There were other children there, too. Although none were injured as badly as Becky, many had been seriously burned and were horribly disfigured. I also learned that I was not in this thing alone. There were other parents from whom I could learn, and perhaps whom I could encourage as well.

In order to see Becky, I had to go through a lengthy preparation. We were not permitted simply to put a surgical gown over our street clothes; we had to take off our street clothes and leave them in a locker room. Before I could go into the ICU, I had to follow a procedure similar to that of a surgeon. After scrubbing up, I had to don rubber gloves, a mask, and a sterile plastic apron over the scrub clothes.

Becky was the only child in the Intensive Care Unit, but two nurses had been assigned to her. They were complete professionals, who had received specialized training in caring for burn patients. Although the young nurses at the Medical University had done a tremendous job, there was no comparison between the levels of expertise. Terri first approached me. "I'll be Becky's nurse," she said. She proceeded to explain to me exactly what was going to be done, how the procedures would work, and what to expect. I learned more from her in ten minutes than I had learned in the eight days in Charleston. As she described the grafting procedures and the need for therapy to prevent scar contractures, I realized how erroneous the young intern's comment about minimal scarring had been. Becky's other nurse was Ann. Together their love and tenderness toward Becky in the months ahead gave more help to Brenda and me than they'll ever know.

Late that afternoon, I met with Dr. MacMillan, the Chief of Staff. He was a gracious and kind man. "Rebecca has a 90 to 95 percent third-degree burn," he related. "Our first concern will be to remove the necrotic tissue and get her body covered with her own skin as soon as possible. She will be under the constant threat of topical infections until her wounds are closed. She has very little skin to work with. That's going to be our biggest problem. We're doing research here with homographs that are proving quite successful. There are various ways of keeping the body fluids in and covering the wounds temporarily."

"They are using pigskin on my wife," I said.

"Yes, and we do that here as well. But we have a large skin bank here with skin tissue typed and frozen. If we can match Rebecca's skin with tissue we have on hand, we will be able to close her wounds for up to two weeks, instead of two or three days." The pigskin would slough off in just a few days.

"Where do you get this donor skin?" I asked.

"I'm sure you're aware of the Organ Donor Program."

I nodded.

"This is similar," he said.

"You mean . . ."

"Yes," he replied, "cadavers."

"Dr. MacMillan, would it be possible for me to donate skin to Becky?"

"It is possible," he answered, "although you need to be aware that this skin would only be a temporary covering, sort of a long-term bandage."

"Look," I said, "I'll do anything I can to help her. I already feel helpless enough. Maybe this is something I can do."

He explained that there are various antigens in the blood and that every person has three or four of them. If those antigens match another person's, then the skin is of the same type, as any other organ in the body would be. The skin is an organ, in fact the largest organ of the body. Dr. MacMillan made arrangements for me to receive a blood test the next day to see if I could donate skin to Becky.

Before leaving his office, I asked one more question, "Dr. MacMillan, do you think Becky has a chance?"

"I can already tell that Rebecca is a remarkable little girl. The fact that she has survived more than ten days is very encouraging. You can be sure we're going to give her the best care that she can get." He was convincing, and I was tremendously reassured.

"Dr. MacMillan, if she lives, what will she look like?"

He paused for a moment, then said, "You've seen the other children?"

"Yes, sir, it's just that, well, I had heard that there are some techniques available now that could minimize the scarring."

"There is a dependable rule of thumb," he responded. "Once burned, always scarred."

"I understand," I said.

We met with the Director of Family Services, who gave us a packet of information and helped me fill out some forms. She, like everyone else, was tremendously helpful and courteous. I received many unofficial courtesies that day, as well as in the days ahead.

My brother, Harold, came to pick us up on his way home from work. Arrangements were made for Debbie and Johnny to stay with him and his family for a while, then with my aunt and grandmother in Elizabethtown, Kentucky, just two and a half hours away. Brenda's father and stepmother were just three hours away. The children would be fine, I was sure.

I stayed with Becky for three days. The tissue typing was disappointing—it didn't match.

On the day I left, my brother took me to the hospital for a brief visit with Becky, then to the airport for my return to Charleston. Leaving Brenda had been hard, but she was an adult, she was conscious, and she could communicate. She knew the Lord, and her faith was strong.

But Becky was unconscious. Although surrounded with people, she was completely cut off from her family. Harold searched for the right words to encourage me. I was the preacher. I had once confronted him as I had everyone else in the family about their spiritual condition as soon as I'd returned from Thailand. About a year after my salvation, Harold had given his life to the Lord and was faithfully attending church with his family.

"I read a book recently," he said. "It was about Corrie ten Boom. She had to take a train ride, and she was very scared. For several days she worried about her fear of trains, but she traveled with her father and enjoyed the trip completely. Her father asked her, 'What happened to your fear?' 'Oh, I wasn't thinking about being on the train,' she replied, 'I was thinking about being with you.'"

It was exactly what I needed to hear. Yes, the Lord was with me, but more importantly for Becky, the Lord was with her. After my brother and I embraced, I left for Charleston. I visited Brenda and then returned to Greenville to salvage what was left of our household goods and to preach in my church that Sunday. In two weeks we had discovered the routine that was to become a way of life for the next seven months. During those long months, God lovingly led us to face the realities of life we had avoided for many years. I know now that we had been headed down the same wrong path we have seen so many others take. God alone knows where we would have been had He not sent the fire.

Part Two

Hidden Treasure—The Ore

There hath no temptation taken you but such as is common to man: but God is faithful, who will not suffer you to be tempted above that ye are able; but will with the temptation also make a way to escape, that ye may be able to bear it.

1 Corinthians 10:13

Chapter Ten

For we are labourers together with God: ye are God's husbandry,
ye are God's building.

1 Corinthians 3:9

Until the fire, our lives were like those of thousands of couples—one endless struggle to get things under control. We were still praying for God to change our circumstances, to change other people, but not to change us. Through the demands of my early college years and a very early marriage, I learned to be a "take charge" person. I couldn't remember a time when I hadn't been able to drive a little faster, work a little harder, spend a little more money—do something—to change my circumstances. Even after my salvation, though Brenda and I believed the Bible without question, we still did not realize how much we were depending on ourselves and on each other. Brenda depended completely on me. And I knew I was taking advantage of her. Patterns set during many years of rebellion against the Lord are not easy to change. Often those who hear about the fire assume that God chose us because we were strong, but we know that He was showing us our weakness so that we would trust in His strength.

June, 1968

████████████████████████ "Dad, Brenda and I got married yesterday."

Dad's reaction to my phone call was remarkably reasonable, considering the pain it must have brought to him. But then, he'd had quite a bit of practice in dealing with painful calls from me.

The year before, Dad had come to pick up a car I had wrecked that was still registered in his name. I had finished my first year of college. Brenda and I were engaged. It was 1967, the height of the Vietnam war. I wasn't into drugs, rock music, or the rebellion of the day. I had a different kind of stubbornness, a willful "I'll show you" attitude that regularly got me into trouble.

Dad had come from his new assignment in Georgia to Cincinnati where I worked driving an ice cream truck that summer. The insurance had been canceled on the wrecked car, and he couldn't let me keep it. "Look, Dad," I said, "just do what you've got to do." Dad turned and walked away.

As I was growing up, I had been so frustrated that Dad would not talk things out with me. I felt that he was always ready to tell me what I had done wrong, but had little to say to help me straighten it out—let alone prevent mistakes. I could not appreciate his struggle with unresolved problems or uncertainty about his role as a father. *He is the parent; isn't he supposed to know all the answers?* As the son of a preacher, I fell into the common trap of believing people expected me to be perfect without realizing that I was expecting Dad to be perfect. *He's a preacher; if he doesn't know the answers, why is he telling everyone else how to live?*

I drove the ice cream truck out of the garage that morning as Dad hooked a tow bar to the car. I looked at Dad in anger, and he looked back at me in frustration.

I suppose he came to expect me to do the irresponsible thing, so when his nineteen-year-old son called him to announce his marriage, he wasn't really surprised. This time I simply said, "Dad, I've got to do what I've got to do."

Brenda and I married young—too young—because we thought we were deeply in love. In fact, we were in love with the feeling we had when we were with each other. I hadn't dated much in high school. I would rather not ask a girl for a date than have her say no. Even if I thought I could get a date, I was afraid I couldn't get the car; it just wasn't worth asking. There were too many rules, too much control from Dad. But band practice gave me plenty of after-school activities and free admission to ball games, and I went after as many leadership positions as I could get to prove that it really didn't matter whether I was accepted or not.

One of my greatest problems was that it did matter—very much. I thought I had something to prove, and by my senior year, I was president of the Student Council. My best friend, Mike, was the vice president. After graduation, we both went to the college that our favorite teacher had attended.

The first time I saw Mike was in our freshman English class. He was thin and wore thick glasses. He was funny, and we became life-long friends! He would listen to me when no one else would, and he had a confidence I couldn't understand. Our grades weren't exceptional, but we believed we were probably the two smartest fellows in the school. We impressed the girls with cautious amusement at our decision to embrace atheism. I concluded that my parents were helpless morons and, in fact, I thought their problem was religion. I rejected it and them. I left home the day after graduation at the age of seventeen.

Two weeks later I was sweeping the floor and working the only paying job I could find. I stood with the broom, beneath a picture of a professional saxophonist, thinking about the fact that I was to begin college in less than ninety days and would be paying my way with a music scholarship, playing the saxophone. *This is ridiculous,* I thought. I quit the job and hitchhiked home, where I took a room with an elderly woman from the church my dad had pastored.

I got a job with the state government, bought an old '41 Plymouth for $80, and saved the rest of my money for the fall. Mike bought a '47 Chrysler, and we packed as much fun into the rest of the summer as time would allow. In early September, we parked our cars and headed south to the little college in the mountains. We roomed together and adopted the role of young, pipe-smoking scholars.

* * *

When I was just nine years old, my parents separated. It was a separation full of pain and anger. During all the important times in my life, I felt that I had to decide which parent to be friends with. It seemed that to be friends with one was to hate the other. I feared the combined reactions if they were together. For my high school graduation, my mother said she would not come if my father was there, and my father said he would not come if my mother was there! I finally mediated an agreement—they sat on opposite sides of the gym and never spoke.

I have loved my stepmother for a long time. She is a godly, precious woman. From the time my father met her when I was fifteen, I hoped they would marry. I called her Mom from the night they married. I stood up with them and signed their marriage license as a witness. My stepmother is not a talkative person, but I have always been able to depend on her to be there. In many ways she has been a mother to me, and I have never wanted to see her hurt.

I love my real mother, too. When I was a child, I could not understand her struggle. I did not understand why she had taken the children and left my dad. I did not understand many of the other things she did. At that time I was angry with her, but I still loved her because she was my mother. The sweet memories that should have corrected the bitterness only made it harder to bear.

When we were little, we lived on a farm. I often gathered cherries for my mother, and she would make us a cherry pie. Other times she made fudge. We would sit together, eating fudge and cracking nuts on the fireplace hearth in our little house in Faber, Kentucky. I often reminded myself in later years of all the good times.

Mom had married at fifteen to get away from home and to keep from going to high school because she had no decent clothes to wear. She divorced her first husband and at the age of eighteen married my father. When I was five years old, a Salvation Army captain who was visiting in our home led Mom to the Lord. Sadly, Mom was taught that you had to achieve perfection. She could never get victory over her temper, and she feared that God could never accept her.

When my sister was one and I was nine, my mother left my father. She took us to a little city in Ohio. There she met some women who liked to drink and party. From the time I was ten until I was fourteen, life remained very difficult and confusing.

My father stayed in Kentucky. My grandmother, who had divorced her husband after forty years of marriage, lived with him. Mamaw said she was afraid of Papaw. He'd had a stroke several years earlier and he was not the same, so she moved in with my father. I was afraid of Papaw. He had been kind to me when I was a child and had loved me and treated me "special." We had lots of "secrets"—just between us. One of the reasons I stayed with Mom was the guilt I began to feel with Papaw when I was nine or ten years old. I wondered if I was to blame for Mamaw's divorcing him. John and I had been married more than twenty years before he was able to help me work my way through the painful memories of Papaw.

The same Salvation Army captain who led Mom to the Lord led Dad to the Lord, too, and my dad felt called to preach. Dad had polio when he was a small child and struggled with a crippled arm and leg. His tender heart made him very emotional, and his handicaps caused others to do things he should have done for himself. He made his living by driving a taxicab and then a commercial bus. Although he could not support our family in the ministry, he managed a small grocery store and preached on the weekends.

Dad left the Salvation Army and studied to be a lay preacher in the Methodist church. By the time I was fourteen, Dad was preaching in a little country Methodist church about twenty miles from home. At the time, my sister, brother, and I were living with my mother in Ohio. Mom thought she had cancer and sent us to live with my father for a while. We had been with my father in Kentucky for a month or two when my brother, Roger—then ten years old—was killed on an old country road while delivering papers one evening on his bicycle. The man who hit him had been drinking. My mother came to get us, but I decided to stay with my father, who was trying to serve the Lord.

It wasn't that I didn't want to be with Mom; it's just that I was afraid. Ever since her separation from my father, my mother had depended on me to care for the younger children when she worked. I cleaned house, fixed meals on Friday evening when she didn't come home, and felt like a mother to my brother and sister. At twelve, when my sister, Sheila, was born, I cared for her, too. I was not a carefree child. Those years on the farm at ages seven and eight were the only years I considered my childhood years.

The morning of my brother's funeral, my mom and dad were hurting so much. They took it out on each other and I was afraid. To change the subject, in my childlike way, I asked Dad if he was going to open the store that day. Being overcome with grief, he snapped at me and said, "Well, of course not. Your brother is going to be buried today."

My mother, who was sitting on the couch with me, said, "Don't yell at her! That's always the problem; you're too emotional."

She got mad at him and he got mad at her. As they struggled with their own pain I sat there between them, thinking, *Don't they care about me? Why don't they see that I'm hurting too? Why do they always have to yell at each other and fight with each other?*

I can understand now how Mom missed me when I would not go home with her after Roger's death. She was angry with me. My younger sister was only seven years old—not old enough to talk to Mom and be a comfort to her the way I could have been. Mom felt I had let her down at a time when she most needed me. I hated to hurt her, but I didn't want to go back to that life anymore—being afraid at night when I was alone taking care of the children. I wanted to stay in Kentucky where my dad was preaching and be with my grandmother who had taught me the Bible and loved me.

Underlying the pain of the divorce, the drinking, and the death of my brother, was another horror deep within my soul. I had fled from my grandfather at age ten to be with my mother, but I could never tell anyone in the family the real reason. In Ohio I was afraid of being alone because of the son of the woman downstairs. Mom had assured me that he would come to help if we ever had a problem. He soon became the problem. I resisted him successfully, but my fear deepened. I learned that the only way to protect myself was to keep every relationship as superficial as possible. I was outgoing and friendly by nature, but when I became too friendly, it was like wearing a sign that said "Take advantage of me."

I desperately wanted to have what I thought was a normal life, so I stayed in Kentucky from age fourteen until I graduated from high school at seventeen. Then I went off to college, where I met John. It wasn't until years later that I understood how God had used those painful years to prepare me to comfort others. Until I learned how to trust Him in spite of my pain, I had no idea how much I would go on to hurt myself and my family.

Chapter Eleven

According to the grace of God which is given unto me, as a wise masterbuilder, I have laid the foundation, and another buildeth thereon. But let every man take heed how he buildeth thereupon.

1 Corinthians 3:10

From the time I was fourteen years old—the year my brother was killed—until college, I wanted to live for the Lord. I attended camp meetings at the old Methodist campgrounds in the summer and begged Him to tell me what He wanted me to do with my life. Did God want me to be a missionary, a preacher's wife, or something else? I loved music. I sang in the high school choir and became one of the soloists. What I really wanted to do was to get married and have a family—to "do it right." I wanted a marriage that would last, and children who would never know the instability I had known. To serve the Lord and be a preacher's wife, I thought, would be the greatest things I could do. My father wanted me to go to a small Southern Baptist school, Cumberland College, just twenty miles from home. Although I wanted to get farther away from home, I ended up at Cumberland that fall, with a partial voice scholarship plus a work scholarship. For the first semester, my parents sent $50 a month and paid for my books. After that, I had to handle it on my own with grants, music, and work scholarships.

* * *

Music held no real fascination for me. Dad played the piano beautifully, and we always had good music in the house. Our baby grand piano was always the nicest piece of furniture in our home. Dad would play while Mom prepared Sunday dinner. I heard Mom say once that the saxophone was her favorite; in the fifth grade I started to play. My aunt bought me an old Buescher alto sax, and I carried it to school every day for years.

Since I had to pay my own way through college, a scholarship to Cumberland ruled out any other school. My saxophone was the meal ticket, and it dictated my curriculum. It wasn't enough to pay the bills, and after a few weeks in the Clipper Room at the dining hall, I persuaded the head of the music department to let me have a job cleaning the music building and later repairing musical instruments. I met Brenda in that music building.

I had first seen her when I arrived during Freshman Week. She sang some silly song during the closing assembly. Mike and I had cringed and laughed at her, but she was so sweet—and so pretty. She too was a music major, and we had a number of classes together. I tried my best to impress her. Once in an ear-training class, Dr. Wortman, the head of the music department, sounded an interval on the classroom piano. I was cleaning the building and taking out the trash in the back of the room. After striking the chord three times, he asked in exasperation, "Doesn't anyone know this interval?" Correctly, I replied, "Two octaves and a minor third."

Dr. Wortman and the class turned to see who this brilliant fellow might be, or so I thought as I walked out the door. *I might be sweeping the floor, but I'll show them what I can do.* At that time, I didn't know it was pride and neither did Brenda. She saw me as what I was pretending to be, and I saw her as a friendly, outgoing young lady who really cared about me. As we shared some of our past with each other, we thought we were falling in love. Finally, here was someone who understood. Maybe we did understand the problems—but neither of us knew the answers.

* * *

During the first few days at Cumberland, I noticed John. He wore a white ski sweater, and his hair and eyebrows were dark and thick. He was the best-looking guy I had ever seen. I set out to have him notice me, and I was pretty obvious about it.

As part of my work scholarship, I checked out records in the listening lab so the students could follow the score to the music. One day while John was nearby I scratched a record.

"Cutting a new record?" He said in a tone that amused the others but embarrassed me.

There had to be a better way to begin. My roommate was chasing him too. John had asked her out a few times, but he wasn't very consistent about it. So, just to be able to talk to him, I suggested he pay more attention to her. I was hopelessly infatuated with him at this point, and afraid he might actually work on his relationship with her. This would ruin my chances of ever dating him! He agreed to talk with her and I walked over to the music building to avoid seeing them. I was so upset I couldn't go to my English class. When John showed up, I put on a nonchalant expression and voice, "So, how did it go?"

"Well, sit down. We need to talk."

I sat down on a tuba case. He proceeded to tell me that he had been admiring me but was afraid I wouldn't want to date him.

I was flabbergasted. I sat there with my mouth open. "How long have you felt this way?"

"I've wanted to talk to you about it for a while, but you've been pushing your roommate on me."

That was how it began. At the end of our freshman year, John proposed to me. He was taking me to my parents' home, and then leaving for Cincinnati the next morning. We sat on the rocks above Cumberland Falls; the moon was shining on the water. It was the most romantic moment of my life. John put his arms around me.

"I don't have a ring yet, but will you marry me?" he asked.

"Yes!" I answered.

A few days later, I timidly told my father and stepmother John had asked me to marry him. To my surprise, she and Dad were excited and thought it was wonderful. Before school started in the fall, I returned to Ohio to visit my mother. John came to see me and brought an engagement ring, a little quarter-carat diamond. My mother liked John too and was excited about our engagement. We were nervous about telling John's family. In looking back, I see why they had great reservations: We were so young, and they wanted him to have a college degree. I was eighteen years old, and from a broken home. When John's parents first met me, I'm sure they saw how insecure and naive I was. When I saw the conflicts between John and his dad, I was sure they were my fault. His parents didn't understand him or appreciate him the way I did. They must have known how unprepared I was to give John the help he really needed. Whenever I felt afraid, I took comfort in the diamond ring John had given me. It stayed on my finger until it was cut off the night of the fire.

Chapter Twelve

For other foundation can no man lay than that is laid, which is Jesus Christ. Now if any man build upon this foundation gold, silver, precious stones, wood, hay, stubble . . .

1 Corinthians 3:11–12

A man who had hired both my brother and my father in summers past gave me a job driving an ice cream truck six days a week in Cincinnati. Brenda went to summer school, and I worked. We wrote every day. In July, I left work one night after midnight, got in my car, and drove the rest of the night to spend my day off with her. We had a wonderful time, and I stayed late into the evening, attempting to drive home that night in time for work the next morning. I fell asleep at the wheel and could have lost my life in an accident that severely damaged my car and totaled the car of the man I hit.

Miraculously, no one was hurt; but, of course, my insurance company canceled my insurance since the accident was my fault. I was too embarrassed to contact Dad, but he soon showed up at the garage. We had another confrontation. Dad had no choice; he had to take the car. It was not insured, and there was no way now that I could get insurance. I wouldn't have a decent car again until my second child was on the way. Brenda and I went back to college that fall officially engaged, having spent all our money on our dreams.

We arranged our schedules to be together as much as possible. I joined the chorus, she joined the band. We went on band tours together and made dates out of our school activities. We were really in love, but the emotional attachment had grown so strong and the infatuation so intense that we couldn't notice that we weren't building a good foundation for our marriage. We tried to make plans for a wedding in the summer of '68, but we anticipated my parents' disapproval, and that posed a problem. They knew we were clinging to each other because we had run from them. We couldn't see it. How would we be able to keep harmony between Brenda's divorced parents and my argumentative family? We just ignored them and enjoyed being with each other.

But it was God Who had saved my life in the wreck, and it was God Who was laying the foundation of our marriage in spite of our selfish immaturity.

Before landing the job of repairing musical instruments, I was cleaning the old music building one evening during winter. The building was unusually hot. I found the thermostat turned all the way up. There was an automatically fed, coal-fired furnace in the basement, but I didn't have the key to the furnace room. I opened some windows and continued my work. By the time I had finished cleaning, the building had cooled off. I closed the windows, but before locking up I noticed the smell of something burning. I searched the building but couldn't find the source. Finally, I called security and we went over the building again, including the furnace room. We found nothing.

The security guard made a few calls, and an administrator went through the building again. Dr. Wortman was in Knoxville with several students who were attending a concert. No one could locate the problem, and no one wanted to be responsible for a false alarm. We secured the building, and I went home to the little apartment off campus I had just rented with three friends.

Sometime after midnight, a neighbor knocked at our door and reported that there was a fire on campus. Immediately, I knew—and worse than that, I felt responsible. Seeing the reddened sky, I raced across campus, around the chapel to the old viaduct that crossed a deep valley running through the small town of Williamsburg and the Cumberland College campus. From a hundred yards away I could see the music building in flames. *Oh, no—why didn't I keep looking until I found the problem?* No one was fighting the fire, but a small crowd was forming. *Someone's got to do something!*

Other men quickly streamed out of their dormitories on the other side of the campus. Several of us headed straight for the north side of the building to see if we could salvage our instruments from the fire. In front of the building, an old fire truck and a few firemen were standing around. The hoses were unrolled, but not hooked up. "What's the problem?" I yelled over the roar of the fire. One man shot back, "The plug is stuck, so we sent a man back for a bigger wrench!"

I could see that the front of the building was not burning yet. The flames licked the tops of the nearby trees at the rear corner of the building where the coal was stored. "Let's get some of the instruments out!" I screamed. After a few moments of discussion, the leader of the volunteer firemen directed his men to try to remove some of the furnishings at the front of the building.

"The band room is in front, on the left!" I yelled. Several of us tried to run into the building to hand our instruments out the window. The firemen stopped us. They were carting out old wooden desks and ignoring the valuable instruments! Frustrated, we ran to the window near the instrument case. The room next to it was burning by this time. By now, the wrench had arrived. Soon the volunteer firemen were hosing down the brick facade. Somehow, one of the band members obtained a hose and directed it through the broken windows onto the wall behind the instrument case while others used rakes and limbs to fish out instruments. We saved several thousand dollars worth of equipment before it got so hot we had to pull back.

When we did, I noticed Dr. Wortman, still in his tuxedo from the concert. He was smiling while tears rolled down his cheeks. I was taken aback by his response. I too was crying, like most of us whose future was suddenly and certainly up in smoke. My saxophone was beyond reach. Most of my tuition was being paid by that old horn. Dr. Wortman's music files, notes, books, and irreplaceable mementos were on the second floor. Flames leaped from every window. His office was an inferno.

"The Lord knows," he said. "The Lord knows what's best."

Though I had heard that statement many times, I had never seen it illustrated with such dignity.

The southeast corner wall where the fire had started collapsed, sending a shower of sparks and embers flying for fifty feet. We drew back farther until finally the hoses couldn't reach the fire. It was just too hot. And it was hopeless. There was nothing else we could do.

By dawn, the building had burned to the ground. The brick walls had been pushed in to keep them from falling out. Most of the rubble had collapsed into the basement. Only the burned-out shells of a few pianos and the tarnished hulls of the timpani drums were recognizable. The fire in the furnace room smoldered for several days. And three months later, in early May, as the steam from the coal bin continued to rise on damp mornings, I noticed the unmistakable shape of an old saxophone bell on a pile of salvaged metal. As I stood there looking at the remains of my departed friend, I did not know that God sends beauty for ashes. I soon forgot about the old horn. I was then playing a new Selmer Paris Mark VI, the top of the line—a professional instrument. I had a solo on band tour that spring as well. I also forgot about Dr. Wortman's calm faith in spite of tremendous loss. We were young; we had dreams and plans. The fire was quickly forgotten and its lessons set aside.

* * *

John amazed me with his ability to take care of things. My father had never been a handyman. He was tenderhearted but had little patience with the unexpected. I had never known a man who would take charge and do whatever needed to be done, so I was in awe of John. I felt there was nothing that he couldn't do. I tended to depend on him and not use my own mind. In the early years of our marriage, he would tell me to quit clinging to him so much, that I was suffocating him. He would tell me to stand on my own two feet and think with my own mind. The very thing that attracted me to him became a source of irritation. I thought he was rejecting me.

* * *

When human endeavors seem to succeed without God, the result is an even more dangerous dependence on self. Of course hard work produces success; the problem is in the definition of success. When success is defined by money, it is the biggest deception of all. At college, such financial success came through my sandwich business.

With $15 borrowed from a friend, I purchased enough lunch meat, bread, lettuce, and mayonnaise to make one hundred sandwiches. Although the idea had been another fellow's, no one else had been willing to do the work. After two or three months of trial and error, I had the business perfected. At a set time each day, the grocery had my supplies ready, the bologna was already sliced paper thin, and I had reduced waste to get by on only $12. I later got the materials delivered to my room. Using an assembly-line technique, I could prepare the sandwiches in about an hour. The men in the dormitory expected me during study hours. They had their quarters ready, and this cut my sales time in half. I was now making $13 in less than an hour and a half.

Selling sandwiches five days a week put $65 into my pocket each week. At minimum wage, after taxes, that was more than the earnings of a full-time job! I had money for clothes, for dates, for myself. Not only had I shown my dad I could go to college without his help, I had achieved a pretty decent lifestyle in the process. With this new self-assurance, I launched out into some other projects. Within a few months, I had hired one fellow student to make the sandwiches and another to sell them. I lost a third of my income to overhead, but I was making over $40 a week on an idea with no ongoing work of my own. Now I was sure I could do anything I wanted.

The next summer I worked in Cincinnati again, driving the ice cream truck. I hoped against hope that Brenda and I could be married before school began in the fall. I had been elected president of the band, and we planned to continue our schooling. Brenda and I had become so emotionally dependent on each other that we couldn't function apart. She took advantage of a blowup with her dad to call me to her rescue. She came on the bus to northern Kentucky, and we decided to get married right away.

"Don't you have to be twenty-one to get a marriage license in Kentucky?" Brenda asked.

"Maybe so. We'll lie," I said.

God was still in control. Unknown to us, the day Brenda went to file the application for the license was the first day of a new law that no longer required young men and women to be twenty-one to apply

for a marriage license. The three local TV stations were there inter-
viewing the gleeful brides-to-be. Thus we eloped—on the six o'clock
news.

I planned everything. I drew my paycheck on Tuesday evening.
On Wednesday morning, I rented a tux. Brenda's mother came down
from Ohio with a wedding dress she had ordered from Alden's cat-
alog for $16. I bought the top two layers of a wedding cake on dis-
play in a bakery in town, and purchased a few simple flowers. At noon
we had a wedding.

Not too far from my brother's home, we found a little garage
apartment. We were just fifteen minutes from Cincinnati. Throughout that summer, I sold ice cream at the construction site of the new
Shriners hospital at 202 Goodman Street.

Chapter Thirteen

Every man's work shall be made manifest: for the day shall declare it, because it shall be revealed by fire; and the fire shall try every man's work of what sort it is.

1 Corinthians 3:13

As Brenda and I look back on the early days of our courtship and marriage, we have asked how we could have been so naive. We were in love with love. Our infatuation overwhelmed us, clouded our judgment. At last, here was the person who would make each of us happy. I wonder how a starry-eyed young woman would respond if her boyfriend proposed with brutal honesty, "Would you be willing to wash my socks for the rest of your life?" Or how would I have behaved toward Brenda if I had really known her needs in 1968? I know she meant all those wonderful things she told me about myself; but the tragedy was that I, knowing better, chose to believe them—to believe that I was already such a great guy that I didn't have far to go. I was willing to promise "for better or worse" because I knew it couldn't get much worse than it had already been, could it? "For richer or poorer" was a snap because I had already proven to myself that if I worked hard enough and smart enough, I'd be rich, right? "In sickness and in health" doesn't mean much to a young man whose worst infirmity can be cured with chicken soup and a day or two out of school. The love that Brenda and I had for each other was rooted in self love, but there was no way then that we could know it. And, of course, my love for Brenda could not grow until God helped me get the focus off myself and reconcile my bitterness at Dad.

* * *

Our dating, engagement, and marriage were a fairy tale. We played our roles well and in spite of ourselves did a few things right. We didn't know it then, but our commitments to each other were more accurately a mutual agreement to be used in exchange for the privilege of using the other person.

The emotion of love covered the pain of the emotion of anger. The intensity of our infatuation grew out of the intensity of the bitterness we were trying to escape. I know John loved me, and I loved him more than anyone I had ever known. But we didn't love God because we still hated the way He had chosen to mold our lives. We took the credit for the good in ourselves; we blamed our parents for the bad. There was no room for God in either equation.

I would never have said it, though John often did, but we both believed that God had been unfair to us until He put us together. We idolized our relationship and gave God no choice but to show us who and what we truly were.

* * *

Immaturity and insecurity are dangerous problems when they are carried into marriage. That summer and fall we learned that we were totally unprepared to cope with the pressure of long days at work and little cash. When it came time to go back to school in the fall, our daughter Debbie was on the way. We were broke. I was driving an uninsured car for which I had paid $65, and the cold weather was closing down the ice cream business. I had no hope of finishing college, no money, and no job. I did have a pregnant wife, a 1-A draft status, and a greatly diminished confidence in my ability to be a husband.

The Tet Offensive in January of that year had every young, able-bodied man thinking about his selective service status. If I didn't go back to college, I would be drafted. I put it off as long as possible. Finally in October, I enlisted in the Air Force.

The military has its own way of doing things. "If we wanted you to have a wife, we would have issued you one" became a familiar statement. I was in an aircraft maintenance class when the call came at 2:30. I was a father! I hiked over to the hospital at doubletime to see my weary wife and my beautiful little girl. We named her Debbie, Deborah Kaye—after my sister, Nancy Kaye.

No adult wants a child making his decisions for him, yet we all must live with the consequences of the decisions we made ourselves as children. Brenda and I were children when we left home; we were children when we married; and we were children when we became parents. We lived in a two-room apartment—another garage behind a house. But we were married, and now we had a child. At last we had a real identity—as parents. I was no longer just a music major, nor Brenda a college student. Now we were real people, and we were making real decisions. We bought a set of encyclopedias from a fellow who convinced us of our cleverness in caring about our new daughter's education. All the things that had driven me to leave home at seventeen now seemed quite sensible at twenty. Now I had them on my own terms, or so I convinced myself.

Just a few more months and I'd be back in school anyway. The recruiter had told me that with two years of college behind me, after one year in the service, I could apply for the AECP program—the Airmen's Education and Commissioning Program—to finish my college degree and get a commission.

In the spring of 1969, when Debbie was three months old, Brenda and I got off a plane in Tampa, Florida, where we would spend the next three years. We had no car, no place to live, and $75 in cash, but we had each other, and we had Debbie. Somehow we managed, and when my first year was up, I went in to see the training officer and told him about the recruiter's promise, and he dutifully sent off for my transcripts. I was shocked to learn that none of my music credits were acceptable! Forty-four hours out of sixty wouldn't apply! That left me with only sixteen hours, and I needed thirty to qualify for the program. With my salary at less than $200 a month, there was no way that I could live without a second job in the evenings. *How on earth will I get another fourteen college hours in order to apply for the commissioning program? We'll just have to save our pennies,* I thought, *and Brenda will have to go to work.*

I took a second job at J. C. Penney's in a nearby shopping center, while Brenda worked at the jewelry store next door. Debbie spent most of her time at the day-care center, but she was just a baby, and we thought this was the thing to do. With a little extra money in our pockets, we compensated for the fact we had so little time together. Months went by, yet we weren't getting ahead financially. That was even more depressing. Finally I was able to buy a car but there were payments to meet, then tires to be bought on credit, and a few simple pieces of furniture. Before long, we were hopelessly in debt. It was all we could do to make ends meet working ten hours at the Air Force base and six hours part-time. Our second child was due soon, and Brenda wouldn't be able to work at all. A friend had gotten into a network marketing organization that promised a big income in a short time. Maybe that was the answer!

The sales meetings were like evangelistic services. We would sing songs about the product and hear testimonies from the salesmen who had done well that week, and then our district manager would "preach a sermon" and "give the invitation," asking the visitors to join the company. Brenda and I "walked the aisle" the first night. And we did well. Fifty-two weeks later, I received a gold ring for fifty-two consecutive weeks of high sales. Our district manager was like a father to me. He believed in me and encouraged me. He was always patient with my failures and spent extra time with Brenda and me.

We spent every dime we made and were deeper in debt than ever, but we felt successful. We had a sense of importance. We purchased a new car, rented a larger house, bought furniture, and joined a health spa. My desire for a commission in the Air Force was set aside as we raked in the commissions from our sales. We weren't getting ahead, but we were having fun. Meanwhile, Johnny arrived and joined Debbie at the day-care center.

* * *

When Johnny was six months old, he suffered a bout with the measles. As he was getting over it, the doctor examined him briefly and turned to me. "How long has it been since you had his head measured?"

"Not since he was born," I stammered, taken aback by the question.

"Well," he said, "I want to send him down for x-rays. I'll call you when we're finished evaluating them."

The report was a shock. "The shape of your son's head will be abnormal without surgery," the doctor informed me.

We had no choice. A few weeks later we left Debbie with John's parents in Georgia and hurried to San Antonio, Texas, where the surgery was to be performed. Although God's grace sustained us and God's leading brought Johnny through, we were so far from the Lord we never considered Him at all.

* * *

For the two weeks of Johnny's recuperation, we sat in the smoke-filled waiting room, poring over the coverless magazines and bickering with each other about the emptiness of our lives. We had been married for nearly four years. Three weeks after returning to Tampa, I turned in my sample case. I had decided to re-enlist with the Air Force. My re-enlistment bonus of nearly $8,000 brought tremendous financial relief, even though I received it in increments over the next three years. I made up my mind to start on those fourteen hours the next semester so I could apply once more for the commission. I spent my evenings at home. We enjoyed our children and went to the beach together. Johnny's recovery was complete, and his head looked normal. However, before the semester began, I received transfer orders to Kunsan, Korea—an unaccompanied tour of thirteen months.

We bought a mobile home and set it up in Corbin, Kentucky, next to Brenda's father's house. I had thirty days of leave before my departure, and I spent all of it digging a septic tank and setting up the trailer. The time slipped away so fast. Finally, I boarded the big jet for California, then Korea. It would be four hundred days before I would see my wife and children again.

* * *

I remember the fear I felt. *What will I do? How can I cope without him for a year?* He wouldn't be in danger in Korea the way the men were in Vietnam, but he would still be gone. That year was miserable for me. I refused my parents' offer to attend church with them, and spent my time cooped up in the trailer.

One morning Debbie bounced out of bed and ran into the kitchen. "Where is he? Where is he?" She began looking behind the counter and under the table.

"Where is who?" I asked, puzzled.

"Daddy!" Then she stopped. Tears streamed down her little face. "I dreamed that Daddy was home." We cried together.

Finally we did begin to prepare for John's homecoming. John and I decided I would go to Georgia to be with his family. He could fly directly there, and they could see him too.

Because we did not want to spend John's thirty-day leave moving the trailer to our new duty station in South Carolina, I decided to do it, with help from some of my cousins. I found a nice lot on a lake adjacent to the base. The trip went great until we got to Myrtle Beach. I had become accustomed to small-town traffic. Forgetting about the turning lane, I made a left turn from the left lane. The cement truck behind me missed my signal and rammed into us. We spun completely around in the road. Debbie was thrown from the car, but miraculously, no one was injured. Although the car was out of commission, it was not a total loss. The repairs would take weeks. Since John was en route home, his dad came to take us back to Georgia.

I met John the next day at the airport. When I saw him step off the plane, I felt only joy. Debbie remembered him vaguely, but Johnny, of course, did not. Yet they had heard his voice and seen his picture enough, so it didn't take long for us to become a family again. However, we didn't realize we were only "playing family."

* * *

Brenda and I had made the classic mistake. We believed that if we could just love each other enough and avoid the mistakes our parents had made, we would succeed and be happy. Little did we realize how creative we would become in finding new ways to make our own mistakes. We knew exactly what we did not want to be—like our parents. We had no idea how to become what we did want to be—happy. We had shut the door to God's greatest channel of help for our own marriage—our parents—because all we could see was the failure in their marriages. We missed God's message because we rejected His messengers. We jumped out of the frying pan and into the fire.

The Vaughn family, Brenda and John holding Johnny and Debbie, the week John left for Korea.

John with Brother Harvey in Thailand the night John was saved.

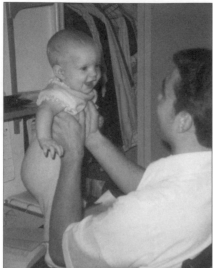

As a student at Bob Jones University, John juggles family responsibilities and studies. Becky is fourteen months old.

Becky poses at age two, one month before the fire.

The people of Faith Baptist Church with their new pastor, spring 1978.

The scene of the May 1978 fire.

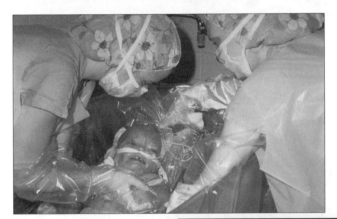

Nurses Terri
and Ann
bathe Becky.

John receives a large
check from friends
at UPS.

Brenda had to sleep on an "air bed" for months.

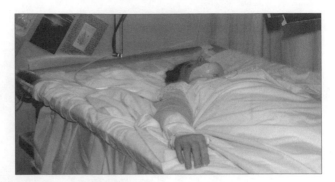

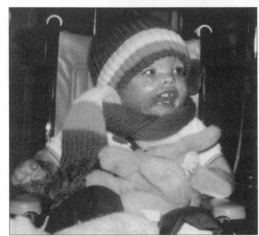

Becky is ready to be moved to the hospital in Greenville.

A warm welcome to Greenville.

Karl Kuntz

Brenda with Becky, age 3, on a follow-up visit to Cincinnati.

Becky, age 5, had prayed for brother Daniel, age 2.

Paul Sponsellor

Becky in first grade at Hidden Treasure Christian School.

Becky begins her
freshman year.

Brenda and Becky as they appeared on
the dedication page of the 1992 Hidden
Treasure Christian School annual.

In 1992
Brenda and John
tour Israel.

Becky is proud of big sister Debbie, receiving her master's degree in 1993.

Brenda and son John at Debbie's graduation.

Becky receives Beau, a companion dog, who will help her live independently at college. Beau was donated by WFBC radio, Nabisco, and First Savings Bank in the summer of 1993.

Bart Boatwright

The Vaughn family in 1994. From left, Joey, John, Brenda, Debbie, Becky, and Daniel (John in inset).

Chapter Fourteen

If any man's work abide which he hath built thereupon, he shall receive a reward. If any man's work shall be burned, he shall suffer loss: but he himself shall be saved; yet so as by fire.

1 Corinthians 3:14–15

It was a long and lonely year. I had completed nine hours of college while in Korea. We were getting close to our goal.

Johnny didn't even know me. I pushed him too hard and expected too much of him. I was under time pressure but still expected him to respond to me warmly in the few minutes I had to spend with him each day. I promised him that as soon as I finished my college work in the evenings, we would have lots of time together.

I enrolled in the University of South Carolina at Conway and finished another six hours that summer. It was a grueling schedule: eight to ten hours on base, and five or six hours in class, then home to a sleeping family to do my homework. *I'm doing it for them,* I told myself.

As soon as I had the necessary hours, I reapplied for the AECP. It took six weeks to process my application, so I enrolled in another course that September. In October, I received word that I had been accepted; if there was an opening in a college, I could go as early as

January. After nearly five years I was back on target striving for those goals that had justified my decision to join the Air Force in 1968.

Two weeks after learning I was approved for the commissioning program, the major called me into his office.

"You're going to Thailand," he said abruptly. I stared at him in disbelief. "Ten days, get your affairs in order."

"But, sir, I've only been back five months," I protested.

"This is a temporary assignment. You'll be home in six months. I'm sorry, that's all there is to it."

There was no sense in pressing it further. I had chosen the military as my career, and if I was going to be a "lifer," I had to act like one. "Yes, sir," I replied as I saluted and marched out of his office.

Brenda cried, and then we argued. Neither of us knew how to respond. "Another Thanksgiving alone," she complained, "another Christmas without you. I'm not cut out for this! This isn't why I got married." Good-byes were painful. Brenda and I knew we were taking out our frustrations on each other. It broke my heart to leave her and the kids again.

I hated Southeast Asia! I hated the heat, I hated fish, and I hated rice. I hated my father for not making me want to stay at home and get a decent start in life. I hated myself. But most of all, without knowing it I hated God.

My assignment was on the midnight shift. I was a flight supervisor, with a twelve-man crew responsible for getting twelve A-7 aircraft ready for flight each dawn. We were still flying air support into Vietnam. After arriving, I reported to the training officer and made sure he would keep an eye on my AECP application. I then enrolled in another course with the University of Maryland extension, arranging to finish my USC course by correspondence. The course was on "Twentieth Century European Foreign Policy."

Every evening before work, I would go to the USO to write my wife a letter. There I met Gary. I thought he was also a student because he was always reading. In fact, he was reading the Bible. While on duty, I met Gus, who witnessed to me regularly. I felt surrounded by religious fanatics. One day, I received a tract about the Antichrist, the mark of the beast, and the end times. That night in my dispatch truck, I knew I could no longer run from God.

Gus and Gary encouraged me to attend a Bible study in town at a missionary's home. We were in the living room of the missionary's home. It was January 1974, and Thailand was hot and humid. For nearly a month I had been trying to become worthy of salvation. That night, missionary Harvey Boese talked about salvation being a *gift*. The biblical passage he read seemed to answer every question in my mind. Then he invited all of us to join him in prayer. We knelt in a circle. Each of us was supposed to pray. I didn't really hear the prayers of the others.

What can I say, how can I sound convincing? I thought. I had never *sincerely* talked to God. *Maybe I can say some of the same things I said as a boy when praying with my grandmother by her bedside. No, that won't do. If there really is a God, I have to be honest. What can I say to Him?*

And then it was my turn.

"Lord, it looks like my plans are changing. Becoming a pilot doesn't seem to be as important to me now. Whether I stay in the Air Force or not . . . really doesn't matter. Whether I ever become a writer or not . . . what I really want for my life right now is to know what You want. Lord, just take my life completely and do whatever You want with it."

I didn't confess out loud that I was a sinner, though I knew it in my heart. I didn't say the words, "Please save me," though that's what I meant. And God heard my prayer. As we got back on the bus to return to base, I told Gary, "You know, for several years now the most important thing in life to me has been to stay on schedule, get the commission, learn to fly, have an exciting life, retire at the age of forty, then settle down and be a writer."

"What do you want to write?" Gary asked.

"Who knows," I replied. "It just sounded like an exciting lifestyle to me up till now. But not anymore. Wanting what God wants and believing that He has saved me makes all the difference. It really doesn't matter, I suppose. I'm sure He'll show me."

And He did. Immediately, my life changed—completely. Not my character or my personality, but for the first time in my life I had real direction and purpose. Things began to make sense. I saw my so-called "successes" as merely the ambitious struggles of a searching young man. I felt a deep, abiding sense of urgency to get back to my family, not just to be with them but to build a proper foundation so I could teach my children about Christ and take them to church as I had never done. Three weeks after my salvation, I felt God calling me to preach.

"Lord, don't you want me to stay in the service?" I prayed. "I've waited for five years to be approved for this commission and now it seems like I've finally got it. What about that?"

Two days later, I received a letter informing me that the Airmen's Education and Commissioning Program had been terminated. The door had been completely closed. There was no point in continuing my military career.

* * *

John began his Christian life as he had done everything else. He wrote home immediately and said, "Send me my Bible and start going to church." At that point, I wanted nothing to do with the Lord. I had been away from Him for so long; I had seared my conscience so effectively that I didn't think about the Lord at all anymore.

What do you mean, "go to church"? What's the matter with you?

For the next few weeks, his letters were filled with "Praise the Lord!" We witnessed to so-and-so. Praise the Lord! We saw this happen. Praise the Lord this, and praise the Lord that.

Praise the Lord for what? I thought. *What's wrong with him?*

I was miserable. I went to the base chaplain and told him I just didn't know what to do. "I don't even know this man anymore," I said. He gave me an hour and a half of psychology ("I'm OK, you're OK" was the fad that year) and told me to be patient. "John will be all right once he gets home again."

* * *

I learned how to call Brenda on the MARS station on Saturday nights. There was a thirteen-hour difference, so it was mid-morning in the states. We had to terminate every sentence with the word "over," and we had no idea who was listening in, but our Christian fellowship began through those phone calls. Having been saved as a young child, Brenda had strayed far from the Lord because of her relationship with me. For the first time in our lives, we started com-municating—really communicating. I couldn't wait to get home. For the ninety days until our return to the states, Gary met me at my bar-racks every day. We ate together, studied the Bible together, and prayed. He discipled me faithfully. When I told him I thought I was called to preach, he encouraged me. We started a Bible study in the USO, and within the first month I had led a soul to Christ. Now I knew my purpose in life. I knew I'd need to finish college in order to go into the ministry, so I enrolled in a speech course. I preached my first sermon in that class.

* * *

John's tour of duty was extended for thirty days in Thailand, so his return home was a month late. Finally in May 1974 he arrived. The base paper had shown a picture of our family embracing as he departed for Thailand. There was another picture of the homecoming. Those two pictures told the story. In the first were tears of sorrow; in the second, tears of joy. We were different people, but we had not yet reached our destination. We had only just begun our journey together.

The first year was both wonderful and miserable. I soon rededicated my life to the Lord. It was wonderful to grow spiritually and learn God's answers to problems—problems we had for years been trying to deny or answer in the flesh. It was miserable to realize how shallow our lives were, how ill-prepared we still were in marriage, and what poor parents we were. John began to see that many of his skills were based on pride and self-confi-dence instead of true spirituality. We both had a long way to go. John still did not realize how much the old prove-it-to-Dad mentality controlled his ambition for the ministry, and I had no idea how much I was trusting him instead of the Lord.

Chapter Fifteen

Know ye not that ye are the temple of God, and that the Spirit of God dwelleth in you? If any man defile the temple of God, him shall God destroy; for the temple of God is holy, which temple ye are.

1 Corinthians 3:16–17

A new conflict arose that was harder than the struggle for survival on a low income or the pain of separation—the war within us between the old habits of the flesh and the new desires of the spirit. We carried our old plans for success and security on our own terms to church. God's truth chipped away at these monuments to our dreams. Like a child watching a sculptor, we couldn't see the completed work of art; we could only see the daily loss of perfectly good stone. We were model students, however. Head knowledge came quickly, as we learned the right answers. As a salesman, I could be convincing with a truth whether it had become a reality in my own life or not. Brenda was as exciting and emotional as ever. After her rededication, we both were zealous about serving Him. Within a few months we were leaders in our church. Many of the other couples in the rapidly growing church were there because we had led them to the Lord or persuaded them to attend. If we had this much influence as members, surely we would be successful in the ministry!

* * *

John's military duty now became an opportunity for evangelism, and the young couples in our trailer park learned to come with us to church or to avoid us entirely. For the first time Christianity meant more to me than just a lifestyle; it became my life. I hadn't always seen it that way. Before John returned home, I started attending a nearby church. Our sharing group was fun. The leader talked mostly about ESP and UFO's, but at least I was back in church. When John attended the group, he asked, "Don't you people study the Bible?" John had definitely changed. He might as well have walked in and said, "I'm the head of this house and this is the way we're going to do things." Talk about World War III! I informed him that I'd been on my own for nineteen months out of the last two years. Now *he* wanted to make the decisions. The Lord really had to do some work in my heart. I'd never heard of the principle of submission, but I certainly got my first lesson.

His first few days home were unbelievable. He wanted to read the Bible and pray all the time. I wanted to talk about us and catch up on the past months. He was putting a lot of pressure on me. I couldn't understand why he was so hung up on all this. We couldn't agree on anything. Arguments ensued and created a breakdown in communication. I was angry that we lost what should have been a sweet time of reunion. Although glad to see Daddy, the children were confused by all the tension.

After several days, I was near tears. I sat on the deck of our trailer, inwardly yelling at God about our situation. But the Lord began to touch my heart, and I wept. I had been saved as a child, but I knew what I needed to do. I had known for a long time that I needed to make things right with the Lord. Because John knew I was a Christian, he rightly expected me to love the Lord as he did. I poured my heart out to God that night and asked Him to forgive me for the way I'd ignored Him in recent years. I asked Him to forgive me for my willfulness, my pride, and my independence. My dependence on John was based on my ability to influence him. If I yielded to God, He would be in charge!

John's change was a spiritual conversion, but the zeal was his personality. I began to change too, but not like John. Slowly, I started seeing things the way John did. We found a small church in Myrtle Beach and began to grow.

* * *

Our new church had high standards. The women wore modest dress; the music honored Christ; and the men were expected to lead their families. There was a biblical reason for everything, and everything made sense. We were getting biblical answers to questions we had asked all our lives. This was not a cultic church or a refuge for weak people who couldn't face the uncertainties of life. It was a place where sensible, logical people were taught the Bible and expected to think and accept responsibility for themselves.

Our families were concerned about us, and our friends in the Air Force couldn't understand us. According to them, we were "going overboard" with Christianity. But we were obeying God to the best of our ability, and we were growing.

In spite of a poor foundation and the resulting marital conflicts, God had blessed us in wonderful ways, especially with our children. Debbie was a beautiful and happy child. John, less than two years younger, was my namesake. Through him I hoped to live out all the happy times I had missed as a child. I would be the father to him that I wished my own father had been. He would respond to my love with total devotion and appreciation, or so I planned. (Years later I would learn that I was not the first father to almost miss his own son by trying to live his own life through his child.)

We had our two children, a girl and a boy. It was irresponsible to bring more than two into this overpopulated world, wasn't it? We lived in a mobile home; we didn't have room anyway. In a few years both children would be in school, and Brenda and I could spend more time together. We needed it and deserved it since our children had been born so quickly and we had been apart so much. I could rationalize it perfectly. It was entirely logical. Two is enough. In fact, for a while I was unwilling to have more than two even if it was God's will. But slowly the Lord began to deal with me about my attitude in this area. I surrendered to him. *All right, Lord. Whatever you want, but you're going to have to tell Brenda!*

* * *

I'll never forget the first ladies' retreat I attended at the Wilds Christian Camp and Conference Center. Mrs. Elizabeth Handford was the speaker.

She had written a book that God had greatly used in my life. During the retreat she talked about the blessings of children. I didn't think I could handle any more children. We had enough trouble meeting Debbie and Johnny's needs. We also had so much rebuilding to do. How could we possibly work on our marriage with more children to care for?

After returning from the Wilds, I didn't dare tell my husband what was on my mind. I simply waited. One day, John approached me and told me the Lord had been dealing with him about something. "Honey," he said, "I wonder if we ought to let the Lord decide how many children we will have."

I should have known. With a lump in my throat, we got on our knees and told the Lord we were going to leave it with Him. In a few months, we moved to Greenville, South Carolina, to enroll in Bob Jones University. Two children, a dog, no job, no house, very little money, and another baby on the way—Becky. Yet because of God's clear leading, we would never question that the Lord meant for us to have her.

* * *

My last year in the Air Force was the only year of true family life we would know for a long time. Before that there were always separations with military duty. The next two years brought full-time school and full-time work. Johnny would be seven and Debbie would be nine when I graduated from college and entered the ministry. I was still making promises, as I had for so many years: "Soon Daddy will be home from overseas, and then we'll have some time together." "Soon Daddy will be finished with school, and then we'll have some time together." Later it would be, "Soon the church will grow, and Daddy won't have to work a second job and then we'll have some time together."

Chapter Sixteen

Let no man deceive himself. If any man among you seemeth to
be wise in this world, let him become a fool, that he may be wise.

1 Corinthians 3:18

In the spring of 1975, our pastor,
Tom Harper, took me to Greenville to visit Bob Jones University. I
was excited about going because I respected the young men from
there who had visited our church. Pastor Harper had graduated from
Bob Jones. Our adult class Sunday school teacher had as well. Pastor Harper had poured his life into me, sharing books and tapes with
me to help me grow. He was an easygoing man who knew exactly
what he believed. I wanted to be like him.

The campus was beautiful. Peaceful. The Lord was there in power.
There was no question about it. After a seven-year setback and two
children, this was where Brenda and I would finish college.

Brenda also enrolled at Bob Jones. Debbie would begin first grade,
and Johnny would be in kindergarten. We were back on track! God
had honored our faithfulness. All we had needed to do was to get
saved and dedicate our hearts to the Lord. The many things we had
struggled to have were coming our way, or so it seemed.

We thought we were almost ready for the ministry, except for
school. As usual, God's answer to prayer about school was taken by
us as His guarantee that all our other hopes would soon be realized.

118

Little did we understand then what painful but priceless lessons the Lord had planned for us.

Managing finances had always been a problem for us. We had no money when we got married, and we had not learned how to manage money during the first seven years of our marriage. Twenty dollars of discretionary income became a twenty-dollar payment on hundreds of dollars in debt. Bill consolidation loans reduced the pressure of monthly payments, but we gave in to temptation again and again and increased the debts when there was enough money on hand to make more payments.

We had started to honor the Lord by tithing and giving sacrificially, and we were learning how to manage our money, but we still lacked wisdom in stewardship and had not yet learned to live by faith. Our only debt was a small car payment. With seven years' time in service, I would receive over $500 a month in benefits from the GI bill for my education.

We spent the first few days in Greenville with a missionary family home on furlough. Bob and Aloha Vance were such an encouragement to us. Since they were changing mission fields they ended up spending two years in Greenville. I told Bob that we were their mission field during those two years. Bob was amused that we had named our little poodle-terrier "Bob"—so much so that he later brought home a strange-looking mutt from the animal shelter and named him "John."

A friend of the Vances gave me a full-time job and arranged the hours so I could attend school. With the new job we had no problem qualifying for a VA loan to purchase a small house just a couple of blocks from the Vances. Brenda was not feeling very well, but we thought it was due to the stress of the move, the new environment, and the schedule. When she continued to feel bad every morning, we remembered our decision to leave the size of our family with the Lord. Unfortunately, I had left the matter of insurance with the Air Force. Debbie and Johnny had both been born in military hospitals, so their births had cost only $5.25 each!

But we knew the Lord was leading us, and He had provided miraculously since we had made our decision to leave the military and return to school. Brenda and I felt just the way we had over nine years before when we enrolled at Cumberland College. Since we would need to be home by the time Johnny got out of kindergarten, and I would need time to work, I signed up for just twelve credit hours and Brenda for just ten. We wrote the checks for our first month's tuition and bought books at the bookstore. We still had over five hundred dollars in savings, the tuition wasn't due for another month, and the house payment wouldn't begin until mid-October.

At the end of that long day of registration, I was sent to the business office. "Yes, I'm John Vaughn; they sent me over here from registration," I told the young lady behind the counter.

"Let's see . . ." she said as she looked over the list from her stack of papers. "Right. We need to have some information about how you plan to take care of your account."

"Well, I'll be getting the GI bill, and I'll pay the rest from what I earn," I said confidently.

"Haven't you heard?" she asked matter-of-factly. "Our new students won't be receiving the GI bill."

"You're kidding."

"No, really. I thought you knew. Maybe you should talk to the business manager."

Mr. Anderson was a big man with a kind but no-nonsense manner. He explained that Bob Jones could not enroll any new students who were receiving the GI bill. The school was in the early stages of a legal battle that would eventually culminate in the Supreme Court's revocation of its tax-exempt status in the early '80s.

"Veterans' benefits are considered government assistance to the school," he explained.

"I thought it was assistance to the student!" I was dumbfounded. In disbelief I managed to reply, "I know God wants me to go to school here, Mr. Anderson. He'll provide. I have a job and a little money in the bank. We'll make it."

The routine of classroom instruction and daily life was a great spiritual help, but on the home front the routine was not so great. Late in September my full-time job abruptly ended when the man who hired me closed down his business and moved away. I was too busy with schoolwork to spend time worrying. Besides, preaching opportunities were opening up, and we were already teaching a Sunday school class at our new church. It wasn't as much like preaching as the adult class had been at our former church; in fact, it was a second grade girls' class, but it was fun. We were serving the Lord! He would take care of us.

We had just enough savings left for the October house payment and car payment, gas, and groceries. Brenda was getting nervous, and I was getting back into the old trust-your-wits mode. The more she worried, the more I made promises I wasn't sure God was going to keep. By November, I was doing a lot for the Lord but not much with the Lord. My tuition payments were already behind, and I saw no way to get caught up before the end of the semester. Brenda began to experience the discomforts of pregnancy, and our bills began to mount. We were now praying for daily food and promising the Lord if He would get us through the first semester, we'd never place both of us in school at the same time again.

I asked Pastor Handford for advice. He told me to trust the Lord.

"Don't undo in the darkness what you saw clearly in the light," he said. "God will test your faith and obedience with trials to help you grow."

Early in November, his prophecy came true. I was placed under the greatest spiritual test of my life up to that point.

Chapter Seventeen

For the wisdom of the world is foolishness with God. For it is written, He taketh the wise in their own craftiness.

1 Corinthians 3:19

Falling back on the determination that had helped me once before, I turned a simple ad in the classified section into a lawn maintenance business with two employees within a month. I was doing a lot of business, and my employees were both making $5 an hour. Lots of money sifted through my checking account but very little of it belonged to me. I landed a job clearing a large, empty lot, and this assignment promised to turn a good profit for one evening's work. I rented a Gravely mower, a large, heavy mower that would easily cut brush and tall weeds, and I put it in an old utility trailer I had taken in payment for another job. The empty lot was nearly twenty miles from my home. Working at fever pitch, I cleared the lot by 4:30 and prepared to load the mower up and return it to the rental company before it closed at 6:00.

Just as I approached my trailer the mower stalled. For nearly thirty minutes I struggled to start it, each time wrapping the heavy strap around the flywheel pulley and straining against the machine's powerful compression. Nothing. I smelled gasoline and suspected that the engine was flooded. It was growing dark as I looked over the engine and tried to figure out what was wrong. Gasoline dripped from the carburetor. Then I discovered the problem. The jet was missing.

Where on earth can it be? I'll never make it by 6:00 now. No way! I'll have to pay another $25 rental fee if I don't get this thing back tonight. What am I going to do?

I wanted to trust the Lord, and I tried, but it was getting dark, and I was alone. As I combed the two-acre lot, covered with shredded debris from the mowing, I begged God to let me find the carburetor jet.

"God, please, please help me find this thing. Oh God, please, please!"

My begging turned to bitterness. "Why are You doing this to me? You told me to come here. You told me to come to Bob Jones. You took my veteran's benefits and my job. You led me to buy the house. You told me to let my wife get pregnant. I'm doing the best I can! What do You want from me?"

I stood there, screaming into the darkening sky. "What do You want me to do? If I'm not doing Your will, just tell me! I'll do whatever You tell me to do—just make it clear to me what You want me to do!"

As I came to my senses, I glanced around to see if anyone had heard me. There was no one in sight. I was so ashamed of myself for being openly angry at God. I fell to my knees sobbing and confessed my anger and my pride to the Lord. I still couldn't understand why everything was going wrong. In my immaturity, I thought that God would guarantee my success and happiness as long as I was trying to obey and serve Him. I had no idea how unprepared I was to serve Him, how much I was trusting myself instead of Him, how much I had to learn. I was unbroken and unusable, and I was getting an unforgettable lesson in submission to the sovereignty of God.

Calmly, without defiance, I prayed. "Lord, I really don't know what to do. If You don't help me, I can't make it by myself. I can't feed my family or pay my bills. I have to have Your help. You saved me from sin; save me from myself."

For a few seemingly endless minutes I felt God's forgiveness and love. I then felt the need to confirm my commitment to God's clear leading in the decisions I had made.

"Lord, when things were easy, and there was no reason to doubt You, this is where You sent me. I'm not going to undo in the darkness what You led me to do in the light." I added, "Lord, if this is not Your will for my life, then take my life. Stop me now, because I'm going to do it anyway—because if I've missed Your will, then it's impossible to know. I almost forgot about the devil, and this is probably him. You stop me if I'm wrong because I'm going to do what I think You have told me to do." Only one other time would I foolishly ask God to stop me instead of waiting for Him to lead me—when I would pray about buying a new house on the morning of the fire.

God's love and mercy were mine in spite of the immaturity of my prayer. I fell forward on my hands and finished crying. In the dim light of dusk, as I lifted my right hand from the newly mown field, I discovered a small metal rod on the ground where my hand had been. It was the carburetor jet.

* * *

John knew better, but I felt that if I could read someone else's book or hear someone else's message and do what they were doing, I would become a spiritual success. Time and again I tried but always fell on my face. I was trying to copy someone else instead of learning from the Lord how He wanted me to correct faults and to put biblical principles to work in my life.

We were told we were legalists, and we were somewhat legalistic in our approach, even though we were not trusting God to save us on our own merits. We knew we could not earn salvation. We just wanted to please God. In fact I was still desperately trying to make God be pleased with me. I knew He accepted me in Christ for salvation, but I still dragged the old baggage of believing He wouldn't be pleased with me unless I lived up to every one of His demands. In my heart I knew I was rightly related to God. In my emotions I still struggled with feelings of rejection and insecurity. John struggled with this too, and we talked about it often. Neither of us realized then that the continued bitterness toward our parents lay at the root of the problem. We knew the problem was not in our "fundamentalism," as we were sometimes told, but we didn't know where it really was.

* * *

I felt like a pretender as I marched down that aisle in my cap and gown at graduation. I had expected to feel educated. In fact, the more I learned, the more I realized how much I did not know. I didn't realize then that an education is an opportunity to learn how to learn; I still thought of it as an obligation to learn facts. Although there had been many life-changing lessons both in class and out, my most valuable lesson during those years in school came through my relationship with my father.

After my first year at Bob Jones University, Brenda and I attended the Institute in Basic Youth Conflicts, Bill Gothard's seminar. We learned the simple principles which have helped hundreds of thousands of Christians bring their lives into balance. For me the most convicting principle was the importance of honoring our parents. I committed myself to honor my father and seek his forgiveness for my bitterness toward him.

In August, Dad and Mom visited us in Greenville. I prayed for the right moment to talk with Dad.

"Dad, I've been learning a lot of principles that are requiring me to make some changes in my life," I began.

"Really?" Dad questioned.

"Yes, and the one that seems to be the most important of all has to do with us. I've made some notes here, if you don't mind, so I won't get sidetracked."

"Okay." Dad waited.

"Well, there are a lot of things that I need to ask your forgiveness for, and if it is all right with you, I'd like to share them with you."

"Son, I know people make mistakes; you don't have to ask my forgiveness for anything."

"I appreciate that, Dad, but this is really important to me, and I'd like to share them with you."

"Okay." Dad seemed tentative, but he listened patiently.

I read through my list and made comments.

"Will you forgive me?" I finally asked.

"You're my son," he said.

"But will you forgive me?" I persisted.

"I forgive you," he finally said.

The relief I felt paralleled my experience on the night of my salvation.

I expected things to change immediately. I thought Dad would ask my forgiveness for all the things that he had done to hurt me, but he didn't. He never did. Following the fire he did begin to show me how much he loved me, and he began to communicate to me in an unmistakable way that he was sorry for the harshness and frustration that had provoked me as a boy. Dad was not able to say the words I said that night in 1976, but that too was God's plan for my life. It was not until Brenda was in the hospital that I began to understand that it was my responsibility to be the kind of son God wanted me to be, rather than demand that Dad be the kind of father I wanted him to be.

The most important decision in my life, other than the decision to trust Christ as my Savior, was my decision to make things right with Dad. It was truly a turning point in my life, although there would still be tension at times after that. But the healing wasn't truly seen until seven years later when he and my aunt asked me to preach at my grandmother's funeral. It was the first sermon my father had ever heard me preach. As I stood by the casket, comforting the family and friends that filed out of the church, Dad embraced me. Through his tears, all he could say was, "Thanks, son." I had actually ministered to his heart.

Two years later the real fruit began to grow. Dad had a heart attack while I was at a conference in Florida. I rushed to the hospital in Georgia where he and Mom anxiously waited to see if bypass surgery was necessary. As I entered the hospital room, Dad reached out for me and drew me to himself for a long embrace. I prayed with him that day and was amazed to remember later that apart from meals and public services, that was the first time I had ever prayed with Dad. It was Saturday, and I told Dad I would not return to Greenville to preach but would stay with him.

"Will you preach for me?" he asked.

I couldn't believe it. I was an independent Baptist. Dad was a United Methodist. He pastored two small churches near Moreland, Georgia. *What will my fellow preachers think of this?* I wondered.

"Sure I will," I responded.

And I did.

Dad recovered, and our fellowship grew sweeter. On the day he retired, my brother and sister and I, and our families, attended Dad's last morning service at his church. He was suffering from myasthenia gravis and his speech was slurred. He asked me to sit on the platform and take over for him if he became too weak. He told everyone about my church and about the fact that Bob Jones University had given me an honorary degree. He introduced me as his son, "Dr. John Vaughn."

It was Father's Day. That evening we went to Greenville where I preached on fatherhood. My brother and sister and I presented a "This is Your Life" program for Dad, using slides we had worked on for months. We honored Dad that night, and when the program was over, for the third time he embraced me for a long, long time.

Fourteen years after the fire, Brenda and I experienced the opportunity of a lifetime when our church sent us to Israel for a two-week study tour. We stopped to visit Dad and Mom the week before we left. Dad had been in the hospital for a week having his blood filtered, and he was feeling somewhat better.

"You get well, and next time I'll take you with me," I told him.

"You just take lots of pictures, buddy; I doubt if I'll make it," Dad said.

As we said good-bye, Brenda and I went to the car and looked back to wave at Dad and Mom in the doorway. Dad followed me to the car. I turned to hug him and we embraced again, longer than we had ever embraced before. Dad had finally learned to say those words I longed to hear so desperately, "I love you, son."

"I love you, too, Dad."

It was the last time I saw him. Those were the last words we spoke to each other.

The day before returning from Israel, we were staying at a kibbutz on the Sea of Galilee. Debbie called during the night to tell us that Dad had died. Early the next morning as I watched the sun rise over the sea, I realized that this relationship was more precious than gold: not the currency of a happy life with Dad that knew no pain or struggle, but the eternal investment of accounts settled, of forgiveness sought and granted, of love restored and respect regained, of years of patience with each other, of that sweet and precious love that cannot begin until bitterness is released and refreshing comes from the Lord.

* * *

As John's graduation approached, we made plans to remain in Greenville so I could finish school. We would then seek a ministry back in Kentucky or wherever the Lord might lead us. We were willing to go to the mission field. When God opened the door for John to become the pastor of a little struggling work called Faith Baptist Church, we both felt it would be a good opportunity to serve while our preparation continued. John might even be able to do some graduate work. I was thrilled to see what a good pastor he was becoming.

My role as a pastor's wife, however, was somewhat more of a concern to me. I was afraid of my own responsibilities and tried to live up to the role as best I could. As the time arrived for the Vances to leave Greenville for their new mission field, my concerns grew. I dreaded it. They had been such a help to us. They had provided wise counsel and a tremendous amount of encouragement. One day just before they left, Aloha brought Johnny and Debbie home after school. We stood in our driveway and chatted for a few moments. I tried to find the words to thank her for all she and Bob had done for us. Tears threatened as I told her, "I just don't know how I'm ever going to be able to be a pastor's wife without you here. I need your help with so many things."

She looked at me with her sweet smile and answered confidently, "No, Brenda. You don't need me anymore. You're ready." Yet I knew there were still many areas of my life in which I was holding out and not truly trusting the Lord. I was afraid He would ask more of me than I could give.

One of John's sermons was a great help to me. His text was 1 Peter 4:12 and 13: "Beloved, think it not strange concerning the fiery trial which is to try you, as though some strange thing happened unto you: but rejoice, inasmuch as ye are partakers of Christ's sufferings; that, when his glory shall be revealed, ye may be glad also with exceeding joy."

As always, his message was powerful and clear. God has gifted him so for preaching. *I'm the problem,* I thought. This was not the usually self-rejecting, insecure response of the fearful woman I had always been, but the Spirit-led realization that I was still bitter at God for my broken home and bitter at Him for the struggles we had endured after John had gotten saved and become so zealous for the Lord's work. I had been totally unwilling to be broken. I was still rebellious. When God had lovingly pressed me to draw closer to Himself, I had pulled away in fear and unbelief.

"The fiery trial is not alien to the Christian life—it is basic," John explained. "So many of us are unwilling to submit to God as He does things to us here in this temporal world so that He can do things through us for eternity!" he preached.

Here I was a pastor's wife! The immensity of the responsibility we'd taken on overwhelmed me; all in a moment, I understood why I had been so worried about my role. I thought, *Lord, I don't even love You as I ought. I still love me more than You, and I still want what I want a lot more than what You want. How can I stand it when real pressure comes? I'll blow over like a feather!*

When the sermon ended and the invitation began, I was the first one down the aisle. John knew about my struggle. He took me into his arms—my husband and my pastor—and prayed with me. We both wept. For the first time ever I surrendered everything to God.

"Lord, I know now that the dross has to be burned away. Help me survive this smelting process. Do whatever You need to do to make my life count for You," I prayed.

I'll never forget that service, or that prayer. It was Sunday, April 23, 1978—twenty-seven days before God put our lives with all their corruption into His cleansing crucible.

Part Three

The Dross

For I reckon that the sufferings of this present time are not worthy to be compared with the glory which shall be revealed in us.
Romans 8:18

Chapter Eighteen

And we know that all things work together for good to them that love God, to them who are the called according to his purpose.

Romans 8:28

I had tremendous confidence in the hospital in Cincinnati. I was able to commit Becky completely to their care. Brenda was in good hands in Charleston, so there was really nothing I could do for either of them. I now had to turn my attention to the church in Greenville—to the home we had left behind.

A month before the fire we had sold the house on Belvedere Road, and we were to give possession to the new owners on June 1. Although they knew about the fire, it would be mid-June before I could call them. Their insurance company was working with mine—sort of. We both had the house and its contents fully insured, but each company wanted the other to pay. With my wife in critical condition over 250 miles away and Becky at the point of death nearly five hundred miles in the opposite direction, I could only imagine the financial crises ahead. But my biggest burden was the sense of loneliness and helplessness.

Faith Baptist Church quickly dispelled the loneliness. In that little 50' x 50' metal building where I had begun my ministry just eight months before, with a congregation that had doubled in size in the

133

few months I had been there, the folks met me with open, compassionate arms. We all shared many tears on my first Sunday in the pulpit following the fire. And I was beginning to get the first hints of
the blessings available to broken people. I was learning that the ministry is a life and not a job!

On Monday, I took care of as many practical things as I could. I
picked up the children's report cards and other materials from school
and withdrew from a course I had been taking at Greenville Tech. I
also rented a post office box since I no longer had an address. I then
opened a new bank account listing the post office box, and I moved
what possessions I had with me into the home of one of my deacons.
I would live there while in Greenville throughout the summer. Tom
and Mary virtually adopted me into their home. Not only did I have
a bedroom, I had a regular place at the table and anything else I
needed. It made the pain of separation from my wife and children
much easier to bear.

Late Monday, Tom and I drove to the house on Belvedere Road
to make plans to salvage whatever we could. I had only seen the outside since the fire, and I had no idea what I would find. The door to
the utility room, which I had hoped was secure, was standing open.
The utility room and kitchen were badly damaged. Nearly everything
in them was destroyed. The cabinets would have to be replaced, the
floor was damaged, the walls needed repair, but to my surprise, there
was relatively little structural damage. The house could easily be
repaired for the new owners.

Even though it was still daylight it was very difficult to see because
everything inside the house had been blackened by the fire. The
flames had scorched our piano. The shades and drapes on the big
picture window across the living room were melted to the glass. The
nails in the sheetrock had popped out from the heat. Everything was
covered with black, greasy soot; we were getting filthy just walking
through the house.

And then I noticed something. There on my desk at the end of
the living room, a spot was not covered with soot. The beautiful teak-
wood elephant I had purchased in a little shop in Bangkok was gone!
It had been a reminder to me that the Lord was my strength, that
He had borne my burden of sin, that He was strong enough to carry

my load. I suddenly realized why the door was standing open. Someone had broken in!

I quickly ran down the hall toward the bedrooms. The drawers had been opened and the contents thrown out into the soot on the floor. Our jewelry box was missing. We didn't have expensive jewelry—just a few silver dollars my grandfather had given me when I was a little boy; my gold ring that I had gotten as an award for consistent sales; mementos really, nothing valuable. But some heartless thief had taken them and kicked us while we were down! I couldn't see beyond the circumstances to the hand of God in this.

I screamed, "Tom, how could anybody do a thing like this?" Wisely, Tom remained silent and let me get it out. Not much else was missing.

A neighbor who had seen my car in the driveway and the door standing open, walked over to offer help.

"John!" I heard her calling from the other end of the house.

"We're back here, Mary," I yelled back with frustration still in my voice.

"Is there anything I can do to help? Any laundry? Can I clean some of these things up for you? I really want to do something to help you."

I had picked up a little pair of Becky's Sunday shoes. "Here, you can take these," I said. I didn't want to see them or think about them right then. My heart was broken for Becky and Brenda. I was angry at whoever had broken into our home and violated what little we had left to call our own. I needed someone to help me bear the burden. She seemed to understand and took the shoes. She collected some clothes that needed washing so I could send them to the children in Kentucky.

I did pick up one item to take with me. It was a little white glove, one of a pair that we had bought Becky for Easter Sunday. I kept the glove in my briefcase for the next four years.

Our dog, Bob, a curly little guy who was part terrier and part poodle, had been lost in the shuffle. My friend Frank who lived in the next block, had thought about Bob, however. Late the night of the fire, Frank had driven by our home and found Bob lying on the little stoop by our front door with his chin between his paws. Frank had taken him home. He told me he would keep Bob as long as necessary. Frank had also made arrangements with our mailman—a good Christian friend—to hold our mail for me. I filed a change of address card at the post office and dropped by Frank's to pick up the mail and check on Bob, who was very glad to see me. It was really hard to leave him.

The stress was taking its toll on me. Everywhere I turned, I was having to say good-bye to life as I had known it before. I thanked the Lord that Brenda and Becky were not there to go through what I was going through, but I felt guilty for even thinking that, since they were suffering so much more than I was. It was good that Debbie and Johnny were not there to see me choking back the tears when I left our little dog behind.

The mail held forms from the insurance company, routine bills, and surprisingly, some cards from friends. I thought it curious that people should want to comfort us by sending a card to the home that had burned. *What else could they do,* I thought as I opened what appeared to be a bill from the Greenville General Hospital. It was for the emergency room service, the ambulance, and the intensive care treatment of Brenda and Becky the night of the fire. I couldn't believe it. They had been in that hospital less than eighteen hours, and the bill was over $1300!

By the time I had made arrangements to rent a truck and pick up our salvageable household goods for storage in Tom's garage, I was being inundated with phone calls from friends. I stopped by the church to draft a letter to our friends. I explained briefly what had happened, told the prognosis for the future, and gave my post office box and the addresses of the hospitals in Charleston and Cincinnati. I took the letter to a printer for two hundred copies.

While the printer was checking the quality of the copies, one of my statements caught his eye. He was standing at the counter when I came back in from making a phone call at the pay phone outside. Neatly wrapped in plastic were my fresh, crisp copies and the printer with tears running down his cheeks. "No charge" was all he could say. "Okay," I replied and shook his hand firmly.

One of the supervisors at United Parcel Service named Carey called me that week and asked me to come by the service center. "Wear a suit," he said.

I didn't question him, but I knew I had to make some kind of decision about my continued employment at UPS. He and several other supervisors met me. Carey had taken up a collection. He had instructed the drivers to contribute $50 each, each of the belt workers to donate $30, and the clerks to give $20. But the people at UPS were not content to give these recommended amounts. They gave nearly twice as much! He presented me a check for $1600. The center manager, Mike, told me that if I would work eight hours a month, they would keep me on the payroll and keep my insurance in force. I worked far more than eight hours a month simply to keep myself busy while at home.

My instructor at Greenville Tech had contacted a local newspaper columnist who featured our story in the paper that week. He had started a fund for us at a local bank and had ordered checks, so I could draw on the account whenever funds were available. Several hundred dollars were sent in as a result of the newspaper article. In less than a month, the Fourth of July celebrations would begin. He wanted to sponsor a concert at Greenville Tech to raise money for my family.

"What exactly did you have in mind?" I asked him on the phone.

"Well, we've got the best rock bands in the state coming," Tom replied.

Not only was I going to have to survive the trauma of my family's injuries, the uncertainty of finances, and the insult of vandals, I was also going to have to teeter on a tightrope of complex spiritual issues. Several people had already questioned my integrity in taking help from the Shriners. I had taken a strong stand against the negative influence of rock music on our young people. Now a rock concert was going to be held in my honor! What was I going to do? The only reasonable thing to do was to go and express my appreciation, as I did.

One afternoon I was sitting in my office at the church, trying to concentrate on my Sunday messages, and yet being distracted by the pressures of all these new, unwanted responsibilities. There was a knock at the door. I opened it to find a kind-looking man with sad eyes. He wore a badge.

"Are you Reverend Vaughn?" he asked.

"Yes sir, I am," I replied.

"Preacher, I really hate this. I really do. More than you know, I hate this. I mean, I've been reading about you in the paper, and I know what happened to your wife and your little girl. I mean, I'd give anything if I didn't have to be here right now. But I've got some papers here I've got to give you."

"Sure," I said as I signed.

He quickly left. I looked down at the two legal documents in front of me, and the words hit me like a fist in the stomach: "Willful, wanton, malicious, negligent . . ."

The parents of the twelve-year-old girl who had been burned with Brenda and Becky were suing us for actual and punitive damages for their daughter's injuries. They were asking $175,000! I was liable for the medical expenses, and evidently her parents were having trouble collecting from my insurance company.

I had considered preaching from the Book of Job. I looked down at my Bible. *Well, Job, what's next?*

Chapter Nineteen

For whom he did foreknow, he also did predestinate to be conformed to the image of his Son, that he might be the firstborn among many brethren.

Romans 8:29

My memories of the burn unit are mostly of being alone. John couldn't be there much of the time. My Christian friends were far away, and my family was even farther away. *I'm all alone, Lord.* But I remembered Scripture: "I will never leave thee or forsake thee. . . . Lo, I am with you alway, even to the end of the earth." *I'm going to have to get my strength from the Lord, not from anyone else. This is the beginning of a new phase in my life. Other people will not be able to help me now.*

In spite of the pain, the loneliness, and the suffering, the nurses and doctors were compassionate—professional and businesslike—but compassionate. I didn't always agree with everything they did. In fact, I often tried to talk them out of many things, but I realized they had to be tough in order to be able to help me.

When they moved me from intensive care to a regular room, I started a routine that lasted for nearly three months. After eating breakfast in the morning, I marked time by counting the patients taken to the tank room. I could hear people moaning and screaming down the hall, and I could do nothing to prevent my turn from coming.

Howard, a male nurse, was a gentle man. We often talked about the Lord as he prepared the tank for my dressing change. If Howard hurt me, there was no way the pain could be avoided. He did everything possible to be gentle and kind. One very special thing he did for me was to keep towels in a little dryer in the tank room. When I came out of the tank and began to shake from the cold, he would put those warm towels over me.

I was determined not to scream; I knew how badly the others' screaming frightened me. Howard would give me a "gauze bullet" to bite on and keep me from screaming. I would quote Scripture and sing songs in my head—anything to keep my mind off the horrible pain.

Whenever my white blood count was high, they covered me with an ointment containing sulphur. It burned terribly, and the pain lasted for hours. Silvadene was the ointment used when the blood count was normal. I was always relieved when sulphur was not necessary.

I sometimes found myself frustrated that the doctors and nurses casually discussed mundane things like their weekend or a funny story. *Don't they care that I'm hurting?* I thought. *How can they talk like this and listen to this throbbing music while I'm in such pain?* In order to survive a job with such intense emotional pressure, perhaps they too needed distractions.

Before skin can be grafted, the burned site must be prepared. Living tissue cannot be transplanted from one site to another unless there is a good blood supply and the tissue being covered is viable. All the burned tissue and any tissue that is not completely healthy must be removed.

The dressing change is very painful because that is how the grafting site is prepared. As soon as I was brought out of the tank, the nurses would apply strips of very fine gauze on the open flesh: My arms, legs, neck, chin, and back were covered. Then they would wrap a thick, soft gauze over that and apply Ace Wraps to each bandaged site. When the bandages had dried, they were removed for the next tank treatment. The Ace Wraps and top layers of gauze came off easily, but the final layer would stick to the flesh. It had to be pulled off to remove any tissue that would come off. As tissue began to slough off, it would be cut free with scissors or scraped off with a surgical instrument. The pain was unbelievable. Sometimes four nurses worked on an arm or a leg. Debridement went quickly that way, but the pain was much greater. Sometimes only one nurse was available. The process was less intense this way, but it would wear me out completely because it took so long.

I expected to begin my skin-graft surgery within a couple of weeks. Due to complications, infections, and my terribly weakened condition, it did not begin until mid-August.

* * *

During my first week home, I took a quick trip to Charleston. I knew I was going to have to find long-term lodging there. I spent one whole day trying to find an affordable apartment to rent and finally settled for a room in a boarding house for eight dollars a night. I stayed there whenever I went to Charleston for the rest of the time Brenda was in the hospital.

I telephoned every day, and sometimes several times a day, to the hospital in Cincinnati. I tried to time my calls in the late afternoon when my brother would stop by on his way home from work. Although the nurses were very open with me about Becky's condition, I could understand my brother's less technical reports better, and he added personal comments, too. Some of our friends from church traveled down to Charleston almost daily to visit Brenda. This was a tremendous help, but it was hard. One young lady passed out right there in Brenda's room when she first saw her.

Our tenth wedding anniversary was June 17. Brenda had been in the hospital almost a month. By then, she knew the doctors and nurses—as I did—by their first names. When I arrived that morning, the staff of the burn unit had decorated her room with balloons and a nice cake. For the first time in a long time we had fun together. Brenda and I laughed until we cried.

That evening, while Brenda was in the Hubbard tank, I received a call from Dr. Bob Jones III. "John, I've been trying to reach you."

"I move around quite a bit these days, Dr. Bob," I answered.

"I know," he said, "and I don't mean to burden you now, but I wanted you to know we're praying for you. I wish there was something I could do. Our hearts are broken for you. There are people all over the country praying for you and Brenda. Everywhere I go people ask me about you. My secretary, Kathy, keeps me posted. She's getting reports from some of your people at the church."

"That means a lot," I told him.

"John, listen, if there's anything we can do—anything—just let us know."

"I really appreciate that, Dr. Bob."

Dr. Bob prayed with me on the phone, and we hung up. I admired him, more than he knew. He has long been one of my heroes. I was proud to be a graduate of Bob Jones University. I not only had my testimony as a Christian but my testimony as a graduate of Bob Jones University as well. These responsibilities were not unneeded pressure, but encouragement from the Lord. God had met my needs over and over again while I was a student. He had provided for our family many times.

I thought about the night that Becky was born in the university hospital. Bob Jones University—the World's Most Unusual University. That was its logo. The film department was called "Unusual Films." Dr. Bob had stopped by the maternity ward the Sunday night Becky was born and told Brenda what a beautiful baby Becky was. I had written to thank him and told him she was a production of "Unusual Babies."

In the years ahead, Dr. Bob's secretary Kathy became a real friend to Becky, often taking her to the university dining hall to eat on Sunday afternoons. One day we had a conversation around our table about where the children had been born. Johnny laughed with us about his friends' surprise that he had been born on an Air Force base. They thought he'd been born on the flight line with the airplanes!

"Where was I born?" Becky piped up.

"You were born at Bob Jones University," I replied. She looked at me with her classic look and a twinkle in her eye. Then, with her dry sense of humor, she said, "Dad, you don't go to Bob Jones to get born; you go to Bob Jones to eat."

The night after the burn unit anniversary party, I reflected over our ten years of marriage. *What will the next ten years hold?* I thought.

In less than a month in the hospital, Brenda had become acquainted with other stories more tragic than our own. Not only were there burned people, but there were also people who didn't have the resources of spiritual strength that we enjoyed. One young woman was badly burned on her face. Her husband had been pouring gasoline into his carburetor from a small tin can. The carburetor had backfired, and he had thrown the can of gasoline over his shoulder just as his wife walked in. As it ignited, he threw the gasoline directly into her face. It had been an accident of course, but her appearance had been changed forever. Whether through guilt or his inability to accept her as she was, the husband had left her in the hospital and filed for a divorce. God was letting me understand something I had said from the pulpit: "Love is not a feeling; love is a responsibility. Love is not something that happens to you; love is something that you do."

Brenda came out of the Hubbard tank room heavily sedated against the pain. I stood by her bedside as she drifted in and out of sleep, and I listened to the screams of the young man who had followed my wife in the tank room. I didn't need to make a decision—my responsibility was obvious. I simply stated it in a new way to myself as I tried to imagine what she had gone through in the hour before. *I didn't marry her skin,* I said to myself. *I married her.*

Chapter Twenty

What shall we then say to these things? If God be for us, who can be against us?

Romans 8:31

SUMMER, 1978

⬛⬛⬛⬛⬛⬛⬛⬛⬛⬛ Becky began having surgical procedures several times each week. Each time she went in for surgery, several procedures would be done. During her entire hospitalization, she would have hundreds of various procedures. She went under anesthetic over fifty times for multiple procedures. She received 171 blood transfusions. The hospital bill for her nine-day stay in Charleston totaled $12,957.00. I had no idea what it was costing for her care at Shriners. I will never really know for sure. The Shriners didn't mention money then; they never have, and they never will.

I made three trips to Cincinnati in June. I flew twice and drove once. Becky was unconscious. Her eyes had been sewn shut. I had no idea if she even knew I was there. It was a comfort to know that my brother was visiting Becky regularly. Even if she couldn't respond, maybe she was hearing Harold as he read her stories and talked to her. He couldn't report much change in her condition from day to day, and the best I could get from the nurses was "She is stable."

By now Brenda was up on her feet, learning to walk again. She was so weak she couldn't stand without a nurse supporting each arm.

144

The pain in her feet was doubled by the fact they were burned and her circulation was so poor from lying on her back for over a month.

Physical pain and emotional upheaval surged in and out of our lives each day. It was so frustrating to try to communicate with each other. By the time we were able to discuss business or progress reports, we could barely remember whom we had told—or whether we had told each other. By the time Brenda heard about the lawsuit, it had already been settled by our insurance company. She had worried about it for days before I thought to tell her it was over.

Yet God continued to care for us. All of my trips to Charleston were made by car. During the summer, I put thirty thousand miles on my car. I listened to the entire Bible on tape. In all this travel and through all the experiences and expenses, I never once lacked money for a tank of gas or a plane ticket. Again and again God proved Himself sufficient to meet the needs of this unbelievably expensive ordeal.

* * *

During those early days in the hospital, my elbows were stiff. I could not get my hands to my face, so I could not brush my teeth, feed myself, brush my hair, or do anything else. Therapists worked with me until I could raise my hands to my face. As soon as I could do that, they splinted them straight so my arms would not draw up permanently. Scarring forces the skin literally to pull itself together, and it often causes debilitating contractions, especially in the joints. Every burned joint had to have a sturdy, plastic splint to keep it straight. The splints went back on as soon as my dressings had been applied in the tank room each morning. At night the nurses tucked me into bed with a neck splint, wrist and hand splints, elbow splints, knee splints, and foot splints. Then they'd smile and wave. "Good night, Brenda!"

One ingenious device was a mouth splint designed to prevent scar contractions around my mouth. I still have problems with my teeth because the skin is so tight around my mouth. As I was healing, my face became very tight. I could not fully close my eyes, and it grew increasingly difficult for me to open my mouth wide enough to eat. The mouth splint was a small, medieval torture device with a thumb screw that pulled the lips to the sides like a child using his fingers to make an ugly face. I still have the mouth splint. I can't believe I actually slept with that thing in place.

Most of the time I slept on an air bed, especially designed for burn victims. It is a large, deep tub the size of a casket, filled with tiny silicone beads and covered with a thick fabric. Warm air is blown up into the beads to create a soft surface on which the patient seems to float, with his body weight perfectly distributed to relieve pressure on the open areas, allowing them to heal better.

I was not allowed to use a pillow because of the neck splint. Usually, I lay flat on my back with my limbs straight out from my body. Oh, how I longed to roll over on my side and pull my knees up for comfort! After surgery on my back or the backs of my legs, I would have to lie face down with my face turned to one side. For at least three days after surgery I could not move. Often I would wake up terrified I might suffocate.

As I got better, my tank room torture would be followed by a long period of sitting in a wheelchair with the legs rests extended. I would sit in the hall with the other patients near the TV until it was our time to go to physical or occupational therapy. One day as we sat there, I heard the nurses talking about a patient who had died in the ICU. As I watched, they wheeled in a stretcher and then took it back out, still empty. Many of the others apparently already knew there was a hollow, stainless steel box beneath the pallet. It took me a short while to realize this. When patients died, this device permitted the staff to remove the body without upsetting the rest of us. Quietness settled in as we sat there contemplating our own mortality and the grave danger each of us faced.

My physical therapist's name was Allison, affectionately referred to as "the blonde Hitler" because she was merciless as far as our therapy was concerned. She yelled at everybody, even the doctors, if our splints had not been left on. And *nothing* was an excuse for missing therapy. Allison and I grew to be good friends. She really helped me in spite of the pain.

Part of my therapy included exercising my fingers on a large, manual typewriter. My left hand, especially, had been deeply burned, and there was a serious question whether I would be able to keep the last two fingers. I asked that the fingers not be amputated so I could play the piano. The doctors agreed, and the fingers healed. Today they are twisted and do not function well, but I'm glad I kept them. In fact, I can play the piano better than before because my smallest finger is pulled to the side and can now reach two extra keys! As I sat, laboriously pushing down one key at a time on that old typewriter, my occupational therapist, Julie, would often call from her room, "Listen to Brenda burn up that typewriter! Hey, if we ever need extra help down here, we'll have the burn unit send you down to do all our correspondence!"

We shared many laughs. A few years later I went back and asked Julie if I had been a bad patient. She laughed.

"Brenda, you never refused therapy, but you always asked if we could wait a little while. 'Can't we do it later?' you'd say. You always tried to put it off."

Through all my therapy and treatment I tried to be patient and cooperative, though I usually made a request or offered an opinion. The pain was inevitable, and I tried every way possible to minimize it and plead with the doctors and nurses to be careful. I felt sure they had no idea how much pain I was in.

When many of my grafts were healing, I was fitted for Jobst pressure garments, which I wore from head to toe, including a mask and gloves. I wore these for a year to keep the scar tissue flat, so it would not become thick and rippled in appearance. While it's impossible to prevent scarring, these ingenious though uncomfortable garments do help greatly. I hated the mask on my face. Only my eyes, nostrils, and mouth could be seen. Had I not worn the mouth splint and the pressure garments, my nose would have pulled to one side, my mouth would have drooped open, and my chin would have been drawn into a mass of scar tissue on my badly burned neck. Today I am able to cover most of the scarring with makeup.

The first time they tried to get me up to walk, I was really nervous. Two small nurses came to lift me out of bed. I asked for the intern on duty or for Tisdale, a large male nurse with broad shoulders, who always made me feel more confident when he helped me into and out of the bed. At first, I discovered my sense of balance was gone. The bottoms of my feet hurt terribly, even with several inches of padding. In order to walk I needed support on both sides. I had to learn to walk all over again. It was one of the most frightening experiences I had.

Chris, another physical therapist, had been there when Becky was brought in that first night. Later that summer she told me, "It was my job to determine what splints Becky would need and to get them on her immediately." She told me how her heart had gone out to this little girl whose mother had also been injured and couldn't be there to comfort her. That night in the emergency room, Chris tried to comfort Becky and talk softly to her. Chris had a tender heart, and I tried to express to her how much her compassion for Becky meant to me. That same summer Chris was attacked in the hospital parking lot. She had a terrible time getting over the pain and trauma as well as her injuries. After she returned to work, I had several opportunities to comfort and encourage her. I knew God was at work in her life. How often I saw those who were hard become harder while those who were tender and sensitive to the things of God become even more tender through their suffering. Chris was becoming more tender. And I was beginning to understand how God uses suffering to perfect the gifts He has given us.

I came to know the nurses fairly well. Trish was so short she had to stand on a stool to get up to my bed and take my blood pressure. Sleep never came fully, and Kathy used to rub my back when I couldn't sleep. This was no small task when I was in full armor lying on my back, yet Kathy would reach under me and do the best she could. Sally was married and expecting a baby. One day when I was especially exhausted, she put a "Do Not Disturb" sign on my door and let me rest without interruption. Even though Joy worked in the burn unit, she took her vacation with a survival team in the wilderness—more hard work. I couldn't believe it. She always spoke to my dad, and she established a good relationship with him. There were two Susies. One was a new Christian with whom I spent a lot of time talking about the Lord. This was a real encouragement to me since I had so little fellowship. The other was a bubbly person who kept me entertained with stories and laughter. There were others . . . Patti, Claudia, three Marys, and a Wendy, who also became my friends.

Yes, I got angry with them, and they got frustrated with me. I wanted them to leave the splints off, and they wouldn't. I wanted more medicine for sleep, and they couldn't give it to me. But they understood and although I complained, I understood, too.

One day one Mary came to give me some medication to reduce my fever. She brought a tall, iced drink for me to enjoy as I took the pills. As she struggled with the packaging on the medication, she set the glass down on the ledge of my air bed. Immediately it spilled into the bed, soaking my back and shoulders.

"Oh, no," she said, "I'll get that up right away."

"You can forget the aspirin," I replied. "I'm cooled off. I don't think I have a fever anymore." We both laughed.

Once a male nurse brought me an Ensure milk shake—a high-calorie drink to aid the healing process. It spilled as well. I persuaded him to leave it and to put towels over the wet part because changing my bed was so painful. By morning the air smelled of sour milk.

I didn't like those milk shakes anyway! The hospital staff insisted that I consume five to six thousand calories a day. Without the calories my body wouldn't heal and make new skin. Pleasant tasting soft drinks were used only as bribes—I had to finish the tasteless milk shakes first.

The nurses frequently told us about one patient named Joe who had eaten all his food and had gotten out of the hospital early. One day Joe came for a visit. I pulled him aside for a few questions.

"All right, Joe, how did you do it? How could anyone ever eat all that food?" I asked him. "We all want to know, because we never hear the end of it."

He laughed out loud and winked at me. Leaning over, he whispered in my ear, "Sit next to the trash can." Then he left with a wave and a smile.

Usually, I was not only in pain but exhausted. I remember how thrilled I was when the doctor told me he thought I would only need one dressing change a day instead of two. I had just prayed, "Lord, I don't see how I can stand this routine much longer." I couldn't sleep well because of the pain and the discomfort of my position.

I missed my family very much. Many times I got upset and often I was in tears. I once pleaded with the Lord to send someone to encourage me. When I opened my eyes, there stood a woman from our church who had come to spend the day with me. What a blessing to realize that before I'd even called, the Lord had answered.

The women in my church were so good to me. Karen visited every week, since she did not work or have children at the time. She brushed my hair and my teeth. One day after they'd placed me on the "tilt board" for a while, my toes itched unbearably. I couldn't reach them, of course, so Karen scratched them for me. We've had lots of hearty laughs about that one ever since.

Other friends drove four hours each way just to spend a couple of hours with me. Many of them hired babysitters in order to care for their children when they came.

Sundays were hard for me because I imagined everyone in church, and I missed my family so much. One Sunday I had visitors at 9:00 A.M. Two ladies from church had left home at 5:00 A.M. to come and spend the day. Whenever friends came, the nurses would bend the rules, letting them all in at once instead of just one or two at a time. We'd sing three-part harmony on the hymns we all knew. I'd do the best I could. I'm sure we gave the other patients some memories!

During the summer John spent most of the weekdays with me and then went home for the weekend. After school started in the fall, he had to be at home to take care of the kids. He would visit me on the weekends except for church times. I lived for the times he would come. I didn't realize until much later in my hospital stay that I was draining every bit of strength from John while not giving him much in return. We were both learning that loving is giving. Later I felt bad that I had not seen through my own pain enough to see his pain. I hadn't been much of an encouragement to him. But God had sustained and comforted him in those lonely days.

I had seen God provide in so many ways. Our bills were paid. Our children were in a Christian school. The fact that Becky was still alive was a miracle of God. There were so many times when I couldn't sleep. The pain would be so great that I would wonder, "God, why won't You take away the pain enough to let me sleep?" At times, I even wondered, *Where is God? Does He know I'm here?*

I had a nice little tape player with my name engraved on it, but I couldn't reach it and sometimes didn't know where it was. The nurses would turn on the Bible tapes John had bought me. When the player was on, I would listen to the promises in the Word of God: "My grace is sufficient for thee. . . . My strength is made perfect in weakness. . . . As thy days, so shall thy strength be. . . . All things work together for good to them that love God, to them who are the called according to his purpose." As I heard these promises, I claimed them for my own.

God, You must have meant this, because if You didn't, I have no hope! I don't have anything else. I found that God is faithful, and when I depended on His promises and reminded Him that I was counting on them, He met the needs of my heart. I began to understand that it was the refiner's job to make the gold. The gold doesn't have to do a thing. We are made in His image, and He allows in our lives the circumstances needed to refine us and bring us to Christlikeness. I was slowly beginning to learn patience as my faith was tried day after day.

* * *

Although Brenda needed me, I had to be in many other places as well. One day in July, I was in Cincinnati. On several previous occasions I had signed surgical release forms and other forms giving permission to the doctors to try experimental procedures and treatments on Becky's numerous topical infections. Most of the time I gave these consents by phone. On this occasion, I was called in to talk with the doctor after an hour beside Becky's bed.

The young intern was very gracious. We sat down in a small office, and he explained to me that this procedure might be a little harder to accept than some of the others. "Reverend Vaughn," he said, "usually necrotic tissue will slough off in time, certainly after several weeks. There is always a danger of gangrene if this doesn't happen. We're going to have to do some work tomorrow on Becky's hands." I braced myself for what I knew was coming. "We've waited as long as possible to ensure the retention of all viable tissue on the fingers. This release is for the amputation procedure."

"How many will she lose?" I asked.

"I'm afraid she's going to lose all of them."

"Doctor, I'm familiar with these forms. If possible, could you just not read these to me. Let me do it myself." When he hesitated, I added, "I'd just like to be alone for a few minutes."

"Sure," he said. "I'll be down at the nurses' station."

I didn't want to sign the paper. I stared at it for a long, long time. *Why do I have to make the decision?* I stared at the pen in my hand and thought of the fingers holding it. *What will her hands look like? What on earth will she be able to do?* I had known this would be coming when I had picked up the little glove from the rubble of our home the month before. *Why don't they just do what they have to do,* I thought. *Why do I have to give them permission?*

In one of the strongest impressions I have ever known, the Lord assured me He was in control. I had no trouble acknowledging that He was using the doctors and nurses to accomplish each step in His perfect plan for Becky. He assured me that He would use me, too. This was my responsibility and, painful as it was, I signed the form and again committed Becky to the Lord.

It has often been said that whenever we commit ourselves to the Lordship of Jesus Christ, He always tests us, not to show *Him* we mean it, but to show *us* we mean it. I walked down the hall and laid the form on the desk in front of the intern.

"Thank you," he said, handing me a small piece of paper. "You got a phone call a while ago. Here's the number." I recognized it immediately as the burn unit in Charleston. The intern must have seen the anxiety in my face. "Why don't you use the phone in my office," he offered. Our eyes met. And I experienced another of those times when one heart touches another, when two minds meet, and when understanding passes between two people without words.

The phone rang on the other end for a long time. Finally, a nurse answered. When I gave her my name, she hurriedly remarked, "Hold for Dr. Ray."

Dr. Ray came on the line. "John," he said, "when are you coming back to Charleston?"

"Well, I was planning to come in the morning," I replied, "but they've got some pretty serious surgery scheduled for Becky. It might be best if I stay here another day."

"It's a tough choice," he said. "I talked with Becky's doctor earlier. But Brenda needs you here as soon as possible."

"What's wrong?" I asked.

"Some congestion that started yesterday. It's pneumonia. She has a high temperature. We've got the cooling blanket on her, but she's in pretty serious shape."

I appreciated his layman's terms and his being frank with me. "What do you mean by 'serious'?" I asked.

"Well, in her weakened condition and with everything else that's going on . . . it's life-threatening."

I had just made one of the hardest decisions of my life. *How can I leave Becky now?* I asked myself. *The least I can do is be with her. But she wouldn't understand anyway. Maybe I should talk to Brenda. Maybe she would want me to stay with Becky.* "Are you saying Brenda wants me there?" I questioned.

"John, I want you here."

Oh, God, what should I do? I pleaded.

"John, get here, STAT!" the doctor ordered.

A couple of quick calls took care of the details. I wouldn't be able to see Debbie and Johnny on this trip even though it had been several weeks. My return flight was rescheduled and one of the Shriners took me to the airport. I flew back into Greenville to pick up my car.

It was nearly midnight when I got there, so I caught a few hours' sleep before leaving. By midmorning I was in Charleston. Dr. Ray met me as I headed for Brenda's room.

"I'm glad you're here," he offered, "but before you talk to Brenda, let me tell you that she is very sick. She doesn't need any bad news right now." I looked at my watch. Becky was going into surgery for the amputation of her fingers in less than an hour.

"I understand," I said. "What about the pneumonia?"

"About the same," he told me, "but we've got a new problem."

"What?" I asked in surprise.

"It looks like hepatitis."

Chapter
Twenty-One

He that spared not his own Son, but delivered him up for us all, how shall he not with him also freely give us all things?

Romans 8:32

SUMMER, 1978

The crisis gradually passed, but as the weeks turned into months, one crisis arose after another. Brenda had to give her full concentration to survival. I was emotionally exhausted and didn't even realize it. Although God's sustaining grace was sufficient, I was physically wearing down.

The church had made plans to remodel our church auditorium that summer. I told the men I thought we should do it even though my family was in the hospital. The church was growing—from forty-five members when I came, to ninety when we had the fire. It was now over 150. Souls were being saved, Christians were seeing revival, and many new members were being added. We had to have more space. I didn't know how to plan properly and delegate authority. There were times when I was torn between going to Charleston to see Brenda, going to Cincinnati to see Becky, and staying up late several nights in a row to make sure the auditorium was ready for Sunday.

The pneumonia cleared, the hepatitis responded to medication, and the amputation of Becky's fingers was weeks in the past. Finally, the remodeling was finished. I took an entire week to go and be with Brenda. The doctors had been telling me that she would be home in six weeks to two months, if everything went well. They would continue to tell me this for nearly four more months.

One day in late August, I was showing Brenda some snapshots of Debbie and Johnny and giving her an update on Becky. The nurses in Cincinnati had sent me some Polaroid shots of Becky, but I didn't think it would be best for Brenda to see them yet. A call came from the business office. The secretary there was keeping me posted on Brenda's account. For some reason, some of the equipment and appliances Brenda needed were not covered by my insurance. The mouth splint, used to help reduce the scar contractures on Brenda's face, was over two hundred dollars. The insurance wouldn't pay anything on it.

At the business office I was told that Brenda's bill would go over a hundred thousand dollars that day and that the computers could not hold six figures. Brenda would need to be discharged and re-admitted under a separate account number. Although I would be receiving a bill, I was assured it was purely administrative. When I walked back upstairs, several nurses were in Brenda's room. They asked me to wait outside. I could hear Brenda crying and arguing with the nurses. Usually she was patient and cooperative. I knew something must have gone wrong. She was still crying when the team left her room.

"What happened, Honey?" I asked. Brenda reached for my hand, but couldn't talk.

Finally she said, "Those idiots said I had discharge orders! They changed my bed and my wristband, and they even pulled out my IV and made a new incision to put it back."

"You're kidding," I replied, furious. This was no place for bureaucratic nonsense. Any fool should have been able to see what had happened. If the business office could communicate with me, why couldn't they talk to the medical personnel? Brenda could see I was upset.

"No, Honey," she said, "let it go. It's over now. I just want some rest." I agreed not to say anything, but I made up my mind that I was going to solve some problems Brenda was having, regardless of what it took.

Later that day, I discussed the heat in Brenda's room with the doctor. It was nearly eighty degrees. The ventilation was poor, and her room was always hot and uncomfortable. Extra heat was produced by the "air bed" she slept on to prevent the breakdown of the very tender grafted skin. Brenda had been moved from an air-conditioned room near the ICU when a more critical patient was transferred in.

"May I get her a fan?" I asked the doctor.

"They don't like for us to allow things like that. Perhaps you can talk to housekeeping," he responded.

"I will," I said emphatically and got the number.

The maintenance supervisor told me that I would have to get the doctor's permission. The fan would need to have a grounded three-prong plug, not an add-on, but a three-wire cord. I looked all over Charleston the next morning for a fan with that kind of wiring. Finally I found one at an electrical supply house for $62.00. It was a three-speed, oscillating fan, and sturdy enough to withstand use as long as Brenda needed it. I set it on her bedside table. Immediately it helped to cool the room. But the fan didn't stay there. The nurses needed the tabletop constantly for things like changing IV's. For several days, I discovered the fan pointing toward the opposite wall or sitting on the floor still running. There was no room for another table, so I called the maintenance supervisor once again.

"We have a fan that the doctor has authorized here in this room in the burn unit. Is it possible to get it mounted on the wall?" I asked with a ring of authority in my voice.

"I'll send someone up," he answered.

When the maintenance man arrived, I was standing in Brenda's room with a surgical gown over my short sleeve white shirt and tie.

"So where do you want this fan, Doctor?" the maintenance man asked.

Doctor? I thought. I pointed to the wall above Brenda's bed. "Right there," I ordered.

The fan helped tremendously. Whenever I called, she thanked me for it. One day in early September after not having seen her for several days, I came in to see how she was doing. I had been busy bringing the children back from Kentucky and getting them set up in school for the fall. As I walked into Brenda's room, excited about seeing her and ready to cheer her up, I walked into a mess! The hundreds of get well cards once taped to the walls to brighten her room had all been pulled down and were now lying on a chair in the corner, stuck together by the tape that had held them up. The tape recorder I had purchased for her had been knocked over into a puddle of liquid where someone had drained a clogged IV tube. On the wall where the fan had been mounted were four holes in the plaster. The room was hot. The fan lay on the floor at the head of her bed with its grill bent. It was still running.

Brenda had been asleep but woke up as I came into the room. "Hi," she said cheerfully.

"This place is a mess!" I exclaimed. "What's been going on here?"

"Oh, I don't know," she replied, "they've been really busy. It's good to see you."

I should have greeted Brenda and given her my full attention, but I had developed a pattern of coping that required my helping with the housekeeping.

"I'm sorry, Honey, let me get this place in order. I can't even sit down and relax in a mess like this." I cleaned up the glucose with paper towels and I made sure her tape recorder was still in working order. The fan seemed to be okay, except for a few dents I repaired. I asked Brenda if she wanted me to stick her cards back up on the walls.

"No," she responded. "They've just painted. It might not be a good idea."

"Okay," I said, "I'll think of another way to save them for you."

After straightening up the room, I sat down. I tried to visit; but the room was so hot and I was so frustrated over the lack of respect toward Brenda's things that I finally said, "Honey, I'll be back in a minute."

I walked out to my car and retrieved some tools I needed to put the fan back up on the wall. I didn't ask anybody or tell anybody. I just drilled the holes, drove the lead anchors into the plaster walls, and put the fan back up. No one ever apologized for knocking it down, and I didn't apologize for putting it back.

While I peeled all the old tape off the cards, Brenda and I visited and laughed together as we thought about our friends who had sent them. There were nearly a thousand. Late that night I stopped by K-Mart to pick up some large metal rings and a hole-puncher. The next day we punched holes in the corners of Brenda's cards and hung them on the traction bar above her bed. She could see them better, and it cheered her to have them there.

As we hung up the cards, the psychiatrist stopped in. He spoke to Brenda and then asked if I would come chat with him.

The two of us went up several floors in the elevator and down a hallway in the new section of the hospital to a small but well-furnished office. The psychiatrist asked me how I thought Brenda was holding up. He then asked how I was doing. I assured him that we were trusting the Lord and doing well.

"The nurses think that your attention to the housekeeping might be making Brenda nervous and causing her to lose confidence in the staff. What do you think?"

I thought, *Well, if we're going to talk about it, let's talk about it.*

"Frankly, Doctor," I replied, "I have not talked to the doctors or the nurses. I'm afraid that if I complain that Brenda is not being treated properly the staff might take it out on her, as stressed out as they already are. The problem is not a lack of care, it is that these people are going to school full-time and working full-time. They are unable to give the proper attention to every patient. I'm simply trying to help."

"Well, maybe you should leave the housekeeping duties to the staff and concentrate on encouraging Brenda."

"Eighty degrees is not very encouraging," I replied. "I placed the fan in her room because the hospital couldn't do anything about the heat. Then someone was careless enough to knock it off the wall and not even take the time to set it back up or turn it off."

"Does that upset you?" he inquired.

"Yes, it upsets me," I said.

"Why do these things upset you so much?" he asked.

"Look, Doctor, I don't need psychoanalysis. I don't mean to be rude, but I suspect you're having a hard time figuring out how Brenda and I are coping as well as we are and how we're able to spend so much of our time encouraging the others in the burn unit. We have a strong faith in the Lord and a deep respect for others. That includes their property."

"What do you mean?" he asked.

"I mean that when you abuse something that belongs to someone, it reflects how you feel about the person."

"And you think that's what the nurses have been doing?"

"Not necessarily, but the two things Brenda has in her room that are helping her are her tape player, on which she listens to the Bible, and the fan, which helps the room stay cool. Both of those things were in very bad condition when I walked in yesterday. I simply took the time to take care of them."

The psychiatrist talked for a while about the importance of not making Brenda nervous or upset. Perhaps he had a point. Maybe I was defining the terms on which I was willing to leave my wife in the care of these people. Perhaps the stress was wearing me down, and it was showing worse than I thought.

Thankfully my fears about complaining were groundless. The housekeeping improved.

We appreciated all the visitors and encouragement, and we gained new perceptions on the things we all tend to say to people who are hurting. "I know just how you feel" became a meaningless statement from someone who could not possibly know. False hope was common as were illogical explanations for what God was doing. Perhaps the strangest comments of all were made by those who didn't know what to say about Becky: "Well, at least you have other children, if Becky doesn't make it."

The hospital chaplain visited frequently, often leaving a little bookmark with part of a psalm and a picture of some flowers. One day I had the impression he wanted to leave as quickly as possible. "Humpf," I grunted, as he left the room. I still had some stored-up anger at Dad and other ministers like him, who I thought were weak. I learned later that Dad had asked him to check on us. I hadn't contacted my parents much that summer.

One day in the hallway outside the burn unit, I met Pastor Wood who had visited Brenda on several occasions. Although she had told me about him, I had not yet had the pleasure of meeting him. We sat down in the nurses' lounge and talked for a long time. Although Pastor Handford had been a source of encouragement to me since the fire, my role was also pastor, and I really had no pastor of my own to confide in on a regular basis. Pastor Wood realized I was still depending too much on myself and not enough on the Lord. As he poured his heart out in prayer for Brenda, I was grateful. But my heart nearly broke when he began to pray for me. I hadn't realized how much I myself needed prayer.

I was trying to take care of Brenda and Becky, Debbie and Johnny, my church, and everyone I met along the way. I wasn't eating right. I wasn't getting enough sleep. I had thrown myself into meaningless busywork and housekeeping chores to make the time go faster while at the hospital. I realized I had some apologies to make to the hospital staff—and to Dad.

On returning to Greenville, I stopped in to see Pastor Handford. Before I left, he took me into a little room off his study where he did his radio broadcast. He cued up the tape of a new song written by Ron Hamilton, who had undergone cancer surgery the same week our home had burned. Ron had lost an eye, and his experience gave birth to a nationwide ministry to children. He had written a song called "Rejoice in the Lord." The chorus was based on Job 23:10.

As I listened to Ron's deep, mellow voice singing sweet words of encouragement, tears rolled down my cheeks. Yes, sometimes I didn't know where God was, but I knew that He knew where I was. And I understood that truly "he knoweth the way that I take: when he hath tried me, I shall come forth as gold."

Chapter Twenty-Two

Who shall lay any thing to the charge of God's elect? It is God that justifieth. Who is he that condemneth? It is Christ that died, yea rather, that is risen again, who is even at the right hand of God, who also maketh intercession for us.

Romans 8:33–34

FALL, 1978

The neighbors who lived near our church had heard that Debbie and Johnny were back in Greenville, and were wondering where we would live. I had been jokingly telling my congregation that I was going to buy the house across the street. Our church was located in an old textile mill village, in which all the homes are alike, and all are over fifty years old.

One Wednesday evening, a lady visited in our service. I had never met her.

"I'm Mrs. Padgett," she said. "Would you like to buy my house?"

Puzzled by this curious introduction, I replied, "Well, where is your house?"

"It's across the street."

"Yes, ma'am, I would," I stated. "I believe God wants me to have that house. How much do you want for it?"

We laughed together and discussed the deal. Within a few days, I had made a down payment and gotten permission to begin remodeling before the closing. Because the house only had four rooms, I needed to put two bedrooms upstairs in the large attic and sheetrock the interior. The exterior had already been remodeled with new vinyl siding, so the house looked very nice. But inside it was old, and I wanted to redo it for Brenda.

Dan McCandless, my music director, was a self-employed handyman. He helped me. We started during September, but there was very little time to get the work done. I had the ambitious impression we could remodel the house in just a few weeks. My former pastor, Tom Harper, was preaching a revival for me in the evenings and helping me with the remodeling during the day. We gutted and reframed the house. I quickly ran out of money. One thing led to another, and we tried to do more than we had originally planned.

Getting the kids back and forth to school consumed much of my time. I wasn't able to get to Cincinnati very often, and it was very hard to leave the children in Greenville while I visited Brenda in Charleston.

In late September, I was listening to Pastor Handford's radio program as I was leaving Greenville for Charleston. The radio signal began to break up as I got out of range so I pulled off the side of the road to listen to his broadcast. He started talking about my family and telling his listeners about our needs. He mentioned Brenda's birthday on September 27, gave the address of the hospital, and encouraged everyone to send her a birthday card. What a blessing that was to me and what a joy to know of the blessing soon coming to her.

Evidently, I had also mentioned Brenda's birthday to Pastor Wood, though I didn't remember it. He had made a note of it. On the morning of her birthday, several of the women from his church appeared with balloons, a cake, party hats, horns, the works. We had a birthday party. Brenda turned thirty flat on her back, but we all sang together and had a great time. It was at the birthday party that I met the Weyriches. Fritz and Erica were from Europe. Brenda was fascinated by their accents, and she loved to hear them talk. They would come and cheer her up at least once a week.

Although we couldn't be sure Becky was still mentally normal, there had been some indicators of awareness. Although her eyes had been opened sometime in August, she just stared blankly ahead. One day I stood by her bed with a little sponge on a stick, like a sucker. I had a cup of water with some mouthwash in it and was cleaning her teeth. She sucked the water out of the sponge. "Do you want some more?" I asked. When I thought I saw her head nod, I offered her more. She drank again. There was no other response, but I talked to her for a long time and told her about Mommy, Debbie, and Johnny. Then I prayed with her before I left.

Later that night, I called my brother who had gone by to see her after work. "I think Becky tried to say something today," he related.

"Really, what?" I asked excitedly.

"Well, I asked her who came to see her today, and I think she tried to whisper, 'Daddy.' "

Brenda and I lived on the possibility that Becky was alert, that her mind had not been damaged, that she might recognize us, and that she might truly be able to survive. She remained in critical condition. Though her body was practically covered with skin by this time, she was still breathing with the help of a respirator. And she was entering her fifth month in the intensive care unit at the Shriners Burns Hospital.

SUNDAY
OCTOBER 8, 5:55 P.M.

The church had planned a missions conference for October 8. At five minutes to six, some of my men, the special speaker, and I were praying in my office. The phone rang. It was my brother, Harold.

"Where are you?" I asked.

"I'm with Becky," Harold said. "She's having a bad day."

"How bad?" I asked.

"Really bad. They're having trouble keeping her heart going."

"What about the respirator?"

"Well, that helps," he said. "The machine is breathing for her and that helps her heart, but her heart has failed five times today. They've got every machine in the building plugged into her."

"Harold . . . what do you think?"

"I don't know, John," he sighed. "It really looks bad . . . I don't see how she can make it."

So, this is how it would be. Five months of suffering. Thousands of miles by car and by air. Tens of thousands of dollars in expense. And Becky was going to die. I had anticipated it. I asked one of the men in the office with me to start calling churches in town to ask them to pray. I had prayed and rehearsed in my mind our plan. I would drive to Charleston to be with Brenda until her father could come and join her. Then I would fly to Cincinnati to get Becky. We already had the grave plot picked out. The little pink and blue blanket that had somehow survived the fire had been laundered and was waiting for her. We would wrap her in the blanket and bury her near our relatives in Kentucky. "She's in the Lord's hands," I told the men in my office. "It looks like soon she'll be in His presence."

* * *

When the doctors called my husband and told him that Becky's condition was critical, I faced one of my hardest moments. They had never given us much hope, but now they said she probably wouldn't live through the night.

John telephoned from Greenville to tell me he would try to come. He was concerned Becky's death might send me into a crisis. While waiting for him, I really wrestled with the Lord. A nurse walked in and put her arm around my shoulder while I cried. I told her Becky was going to die. This was the only time I ever remember being really angry, not that Becky was going to die—I had settled that. I was angry I couldn't be with her. I lay there in the hospital, so helpless. There wasn't a thing I could do. *Lord, why? Why do You have me in this situation? I've tried to do right! If Becky ever needed me, Lord, she needs me now! If she dies I can't even go to the funeral! It's not fair.* I just wanted to be with her, to say some last words to her, to tell her I loved her just one last time. But I couldn't.

But the Lord seemed to say to me, "Brenda, I am there. I will be with Becky. You couldn't do anything for her. I can. I love her more than you do." I had never thought about the Lord loving my children more than I did. I had to place Becky in the Lord's arms that night and ask Him to take care of her.

* * *

We went on with the missions service. Since I wasn't preaching, I prayed during most of it. At the end, I called my brother again. No change. I called the hospital throughout the night. No change. The next day . . . no change! Every day that week the report was the same. The phone bills had been running over $200 a month; this month's would be the biggest yet. I called Brenda with repeated updates since I did not go to Charleston.

On Friday, I phoned Becky's nurse. "Terri, look, we thought Becky was going to die on Sunday, and all this week I've been told there's no change in her condition. What's going on?"

"Well," she replied, "I don't want to give you hope for something that isn't going to happen, and really she isn't noticeably better. If this makes any sense, though, she doesn't seem to be as bad as she was on Sunday."

Her words encouraged me, and I tried to relay this same encouragement to Brenda without raising her expectations too high. She understood. And, slowly Becky improved.

As October wore on, finances got terribly tight. One day while I was working on the house and praying that God would provide money for me to buy materials, a man stopped by. He told me that he was taking a vacation with his family to Florida, and he wanted to give me an amount equal to what he expected to spend. With that, he handed me a check for one thousand dollars. God continued to provide. Since the church was growing the congregation gave me an increase in salary—they were doing all they could. With the Christmas season coming on, my boss at UPS offered me more work. He was very understanding of my pressures. Because I needed the money, I often worked a full forty-hour week.

The day came to close the sale on the new house. Even though I had arranged to purchase the house in my name only, the papers required Brenda's signature. There was no way to get around it; I had to take the papers to Charleston. I left around dark, arrived very late, and went in long enough to get her signature and have it notarized. On the return trip, I was afraid I would fall asleep. I crested a hill and passed a state trooper parked on the shoulder. He pulled me over, and the truck I had been following went on. I had no idea how fast I had been going, and I had only seventeen dollars in my pocket. The trooper said the fine would be twenty.

When I explained where I had been, and why, and that I didn't have twenty dollars, he said, "Oh man, I wish I hadn't written the ticket. Make it ten and take it easy."

I was torn between a sincere desire to be submissive to the sovereign control of God and intense frustration at the unbelievable pressures God was permitting me to face. Every time I seemed to get things under control, something else would happen, some new crisis, some new expense. God had provided so much through so many people that I almost felt the laws didn't apply to me anymore. Now, a speeding ticket! I was almost beginning to expect being treated as the exception to the rules—to get the extra break. I didn't know how much longer I could keep it up.

Chapter
Twenty-Three

Who shall separate us from the love of Christ? shall tribulation, or distress, or persecution, or famine, or nakedness, or peril, or sword?

Romans 8:35

NOVEMBER, 1978

At last in early November, the doctors told Brenda that she would have one more surgery and, if the grafts healed properly, she could come home. No more six-week projections—this meant only three! Brenda wanted to be home for Johnny's birthday and Thanksgiving.

I still foolishly thought that I could have the house finished by then. I worked feverishly to get it done, but every new job led to another. In order to put up new sheetrock, we had reframed most of the walls. After opening the walls, we realized the wiring had to be replaced. Since we were adding some bathrooms, we had to install new plumbing. The condition of the old plumbing was so poor we had to replace it, too. Since sheetrock wasn't available just anywhere, my dad rented a truck and hauled in enough to refinish the entire house. Yet with all the things that lay ahead, the sheetrock would lie stacked on the kitchen floor for months.

* * *

My only view consisted of a brick wall outside my room. The burn unit was isolated because of the danger of contamination and infections. Everything was sterilized or disposable. The patients were not allowed to leave the unit. My world consisted of one hallway and rooms on either side.

I had hoped that I would be home by my birthday in September; but, of course, I was not. I was so desperate to go home that I dreamed about such simple things as going grocery shopping and choosing a head of cabbage. Every day I asked the doctor when I could go home. Although I tried to cooperate, I still wanted to be in control and have a part in the decisions. The bout with hepatitis and pneumonia had set me back for a while. We could do nothing but wait. Then the answer was "possibly October," but the pneumonia returned, and again I faced a setback. November was the next target. I wanted desperately to be home for Johnny's birthday on the 23rd. Johnny had been praying that his mommy would get home for Thanksgiving. This became my prayer too.

When discouragement would set in, I would reason with myself (as I knew John often did with me):

Is the omnipotent God in control?—Yes. Does He love me not based on how I feel, but based on His Word?—Yes. Will He do right?—Yes, of course. Genesis says, "Shall not the God of all the earth do right?"

This would stabilize my thinking and settle my fears, and God would give me the grace to face another day. I had learned not to live in the world of "if only's": *If only I had watched Becky more closely that night . . . If only I had shut the utility room door . . . If only I could go back.* It gave the devil delight to get me thinking that way. I was coming to understand that God was in control whenever I pondered His Word. There were times when I had nothing else—no visitors, no comforters, no hope from the doctors. Yet when all I had was the Word of God, I found that it was all I needed.

Being in the hospital was awful, but I learned to think of it as I thought of having my children. I never enjoyed labor. I would never plan a party for my due date. Each time, I feared I was going to die. But, when the doctor finally put the baby in my arms, I never failed to love the baby because of the pain. Instead, I realized that the pain had brought the baby. The fire became the "labor pain" of our lives. Our lives would not be what they are today, had it not been for the experiences we suffered.

In early November I believed that my "due date" had finally come. The doctor said it was possible. He scheduled my seventh surgery for early that month. It would be my final grafting procedure. If all went well, I could go home a couple of weeks after the surgery.

The day of surgery arrived. As I was wheeled down the hall, the nurses cheered for me. "This is it, Brenda!" they exclaimed.

Oh, how I hoped so!

* * *

Brenda's surgery was a success. Initially the graft looked good; we expected it to take. But an embarrassing and extremely frustrating experience set her back severely. A big, gruff fellow named Reno had given the nurses a fit in another room. As a result, the edge of a bedpan was left to rub against the new graft for nearly three hours. The graft on the back of Brenda's thigh couldn't survive.

* * *

After the surgery, I had to lie on my stomach for three days. I had done it before, but it was a miserable experience. The sheets on the air bed billowed up around my face. I was in constant fear of suffocation. I could not get my hands up to my face because of the splints. The only thing I could do was turn my head from side to side.

When feeding time came, the nurses pressed an area of the bed down beside my face. While holding it there, they would turn the compressor off. The bed immediately became rock hard. They would feed me through the indentation remaining by my mouth. Eating this way caused terrible cramps in my neck. John would often rub my neck to help ease the cramps.

At the end of the third day the doctor turned me over, checked the graft, and said it looked good. He wanted to place me on my face one more day, but I begged him to leave me on my back. "I'll be careful," I promised.

That day was during a weekend. The hospital was always understaffed on the weekends, and there was no one to help me. I was left in a position that hurt the graft.

When he checked it the next day, the doctor shook his head. "The graft is gone," he said. "I don't understand."

"What do you mean, 'It's gone'?" I was incredulous.

"Brenda, I don't know . . . it didn't take."

"What does this mean?" I asked, afraid to hear his answer.

"You know this means a couple of weeks for the donor site to heal so we can harvest the skin again, and then back to surgery . . . then another two weeks of recovery."

"So I won't go home until Christmas."

"Probably not."

I hit bottom. "I quit," I said. But I don't know how I thought I was going to quit. I couldn't just get up out of the bed, go home, and say, "I've had enough of this."

I cried for a long, long time. The hospital called the Weyriches who postponed a birthday celebration planned for their son and immediately drove twenty miles to the hospital. Fritz and Erica entered the room to find me lying on my stomach, sobbing my heart out. Erica put her arm around me. Fritz spoke first.

"Brenda, you're going to be all right."

"No, I'm not. I quit."

"No, you're not quitting."

"Yes, I am."

"No, you can't quit. You're going to get well."

Back and forth we went for some time. Finally, Fritz convinced me the Lord loved me and that even then, nothing was out of His control.

Okay, Lord, I'm no longer in control. I'm not going to ask the therapists to wait till later. I'll do what I'm told. I'll be here as long as You say. And I'll go home when you tell me.

I never asked again when I could go home.

* * *

When I arrived after the graft had sloughed off, Brenda was completely broken. She had been so cooperative and seldom complained when I was there. Of course, she saw it differently.

"I'm through fighting this thing on my terms," Brenda told me when I arrived. "I'm not going to tell the doctors where to put the needles, or how deep, or when. I'm no longer going to make demands during dressing changes. I have surrendered this ordeal completely to the Lord. No more expectations, no more anticipation. I'll get out of here when God is ready for me to get out. And if I never get out of here, that's fine."

She hadn't given up; she had given in. It was a wise decision, spiritually, but her doctors were concerned about a spirit of resignation. They knew she had been looking forward to going home.

* * *

About ten days later, the doctor asked to see me. "How would you like to go home?"

I was shocked. "What do you mean?"

"I think, for the sake of your morale, that you need to go home for a while. I've told John enough about your care that I think he can deal with it for a few days. I think some time with your family will do you good."

I was excited, but fearful. I hadn't anticipated going home in a wheelchair, and not being able to care for my family. I guess I'd thought that once I was home, I would be my old self. I was a little frightened. John encouraged me and came the next weekend to take me home.

* * *

"We'll make it work," I told the doctor.

Brenda was apprehensive. "Where will we stay? The house isn't ready, is it?" she asked.

"We're still with the McCandlesses. The children have beds upstairs with Scott and Shelly. I have a bedroom downstairs. You can share that with me. I'm sure Dan and Sharon won't mind. Let's give it a try."

So the arrangements were made. I had purchased a station wagon to help with all the equipment and supplies we would be carrying around as we visited Becky in Cincinnati. Getting Brenda discharged from the hospital was an ordeal, and it took several hours just to transport her from the room into the car. The ride to Greenville, normally a three-and-a-half to four-hour trip, required six. By the time we got back to Greenville late that evening, Brenda was miserable. It took me two hours to change her dressings and get her into bed.

And we really weren't all back together. Becky wasn't home, and Debbie and Johnny were in school. Brenda needed all of my attention. I couldn't work on the house, I couldn't work at church. For ten days, practically all I did was care for her.

In addition, the insurance would not cover the expenses of her outpatient care. The bandages and medicine alone cost $50 a day. I didn't see how I could handle it. For two hours in the morning, then again two hours in the evening, I carefully unwrapped her dressings, poured vitamin E oil on the open wounds, then wrapped her up again from head to toe. The bandages I removed each day filled a large plastic trash bag. From five until eight in the morning I worked at UPS; then I returned home to help Brenda most of the day. I ignored the church completely.

Brenda was losing so much blood. I was sure she must be anemic. I tried to build up her strength by pumping her full of vitamins. The hospital had made her eat a lot so I thought, *Maybe she's not eating enough.* I went to the grocery store and bought a big package of calves' liver, a food she usually loves. Sharon fixed it, and I urged her to eat it, "Please, Honey, this will help. It'll make you feel better."

Brenda was crying as she tried to sit up in her wheelchair. "Just take me back to the hospital."

"Are you sure?"

"Just take me back," she sobbed.

"Let's just try it a little while longer."

"Honey, take me now."

"Right now?" I asked.

"Right now," she replied.

I thought she was going to pass out so I drove her to the Greenville General Hospital. The emergency room nurse came out and checked her blood pressure and temperature. Her temperature was 103° and her blood pressure was weak.

A young doctor advised me, "By the time we could get her admitted and on the proper IV's, you could have her nearly to Charleston. I'll give her some medication now, but I want you to go straight to the Medical University."

By the time we left it was 9:00 P.M. By midnight, she was back in the burn unit. I sat in the hall feeling like a helpless fool, not knowing what to do next.

Chapter
Twenty-Four

As it is written, For thy sake we are killed all the day long; we are accounted as sheep for the slaughter. Nay, in all these things we are more than conquerors through him that loved us.

Romans 8:36–37

DECEMBER, 1978

The next afternoon, Brenda's fever had broken. The antibiotics from her IV were helping. She was back on the cooling blanket and feeling much better. *This is where she needs to be,* I thought. *I can't give her the care she needs.*

The doctor greeted me warmly.

"Six more weeks, huh, Doc," I said dryly.

"Well, maybe not," he answered. "This infection is coming under control. We'll have to keep her on antibiotics for at least seven days to knock it out; then we'll have a better idea."

"What about her surgery? What about those grafts that didn't take?"

"Evidently, you've done a pretty good job," he said encouragingly. "Her wounds have cleared up more in the last ten days than any of us imagined possible. I don't think she's going to need surgery again."

"Really?" I responded, almost afraid to hope.

"Really," he affirmed. "What have you been doing, anyway?"

"You promise not to scold me?"

"You don't have to tell me if you don't want to," he said, "if it's something other than we told you to do; but whatever it was, it worked."

"Let's just leave it at that," I stated. "I did mostly what you folks told me to, but added a few extra little things, too."

Later at the Shriners hospital, I asked Dr. McMillan if they had ever tried vitamin E. "Sure, we have," he declared, "we've tried everything."

"Do you think it works?" I wanted to know.

"Sometimes."

"I used it on Brenda, and it worked wonders. I was wondering about trying it on Becky."

"It's worth a try. We don't prescribe it here because we have more consistent results with topical steroids. Some people think vitamin E is a miracle cure, but that's unreasonable. However if you get good results, you ought to use it. Sometimes it works and sometimes it doesn't."

Our friends had given us every "miracle cure" in the book. We had been told that if we had put Becky in ice water immediately after the fire, she wouldn't have been scarred. Others told us that we should pour honey on her body, wrap her up and leave the dressings on until they fell off by themselves. Sincere, Bible-believing Christians offered dozens and dozens of home remedies. One family, who owned a health food store, was a tremendous help. They gave us all the vitamins we needed for Brenda after she came home. We probably overdid it, but I believe the vitamins really helped.

*   *   *

The trip home had been exciting for me. I hadn't been outdoors since May. Just seeing the trees and houses and stopping to get a hamburger was thrilling! When I reached home, Sharon had prepared a big meal, but I was so exhausted I had to go to bed.

I soon began to realize how impossible the situation was. When John put me in all my splints, I couldn't even get up to go to the bathroom. I couldn't dress myself. I couldn't do anything for the children. I had to stay in bed except for dressing changes. A throw rug on the floor was enough to trip me up and make me fall. I began to get very frustrated.

John was patient and loving. He had done his best and was broken-hearted when I went back to the hospital. I tried not to let him see how much more secure I felt there. Neither of us realized then that this would become a perfect illustration of how God put us right where He wanted us hundreds of times in the future.

* * *

We had seen so many burn victims and observed the way they either coped or failed to cope. Reno, the patient who had given the nurses such a fit, was still in the hospital. He was big and burly with tattoos on his arms and a thick beard. He had wrecked his motorcycle and when the gas tank blew up, his legs and torso had been badly burned. I had tried to share the Lord with him several times when he first arrived. But he could not accept the fact he was now so dependent. Another patient had been burned in a fight with his ex-wife. She had thrown lye on his face and torso. The man talked incessantly about getting out of the hospital and killing her. Another young girl had suffered a seizure in front of the gas stove while cooking supper. She had almost destroyed her hand by holding it in the flame of the burner. An old man, who eventually died, had been severely burned when someone had lowered him into a tub of scalding water without checking the temperature. Another fellow was burned when the hose he was using to fill his asphalt truck had ruptured, covering him with molten tar. One was electrocuted while working on a high tension wire tower. This man died, and so did many others.

The more we saw, the more we understood the significance of a previous incident in Cincinnati with Becky. Becky's blood gases had to be checked every few hours, and the blood samples were taken from her feet, among the few small areas on her body that were not burned. She had been wearing tennis shoes on the night of the fire. The multitude of tests made her toes look like marked-up pincushions. One day an intern was having trouble getting the blood sample. Stooping over the little bed, he released Becky's foot for a moment to make an adjustment to his equipment. Though as far as we knew Becky was still unconscious, she immediately kicked him squarely in the face—and she kicked hard.

"Wow," the man exclaimed, rubbing his cheekbone. "She's a fighter."

Not all patients were. Reno appeared to be, but not in the right way. He fought reality. He would not accept his injury, and those that didn't accept it didn't make it. During the summer I had tried to talk to Reno while Brenda was in the tank room. He turned toward me and vomited on the floor at my feet. I don't know if the act was deliberate, though the nurses insisted it was. When Brenda was readmitted in December, Reno was in intensive care. He had been losing weight rapidly and was down from two hundred pounds to almost eighty. A trach tube in his throat prevented him from speaking. He was ready to listen.

"Reno, I've been praying for you." He stared at me with sunken eyes. "I know you're pretty sick, but I want you to know that the Lord loves you and He wants to help you." He looked like a desperate man. "Can you hear me?"

No response.

"If you can hear me, blink your eyes," I ordered.

He blinked.

"Reno, can I talk to you about the Lord now? If you want me to, just blink your eyes."

He blinked again.

"All right, here's how we'll do this. If you understand me, or you agree, blink once. If you don't understand me, or you don't agree, blink twice. Understand?"

He blinked once.

As carefully and completely as I could, I told him about the plan of salvation. I told him how and why Jesus Christ had come to die in his place. Then I read him a passage from 1 John: " 'And this is the record, that God hath given to us eternal life, and this life is in his Son. He that hath the Son hath life; and he that hath not the Son of God hath not life. These things have I written unto you that believe on the name of the Son of God; that ye may know that ye have eternal life, and that ye may believe on the name of the Son of God' (1 John 5:11–13). Do you understand what I'm reading?"

He blinked his eyes once.

"Listen to this now. 'If thou shalt confess with thy mouth the Lord Jesus, and shalt believe in thine heart that God hath raised him from the dead, thou shalt be saved. For with the heart man believeth unto righteousness; and with the mouth confession is made unto salvation' (Rom. 10:9–10). Reno, I'm going to ask you some questions. I'll stop at each question and read a verse of Scripture. I want to make sure you understand each step of the way."

" 'For all have sinned, and come short of the glory of God' (Rom. 3:23). Do you admit that you are a sinner?"

Reno blinked his eyes once.

" 'For the wages of sin is death; but the gift of God is eternal life through Jesus Christ our Lord' (Rom. 6:23). Do you realize that because of your sin, you will die eternally (go to hell) unless you are saved?"

He responded that he did.

" 'For by grace are ye saved through faith; and that not of your-selves: it is the gift of God: not of works, lest any man should boast' (Eph. 2:8–9). Do you understand that you cannot save yourself?"

After a moment, he blinked again.

" 'But God commendeth his love toward us, in that, while we were yet sinners, Christ died for us' (Rom. 5:8). Do you believe Christ died in your place?"

He quickly responded.

" 'For God so loved the world, that he gave his only begotten Son, that whosoever believeth in him should not perish, but have ever-lasting life' (John 3:16). Will you receive Him right now?"

The man just stared at me for a time, perhaps struggling to believe that it was so simple.

"Do you want to receive Christ as your Savior?"

One blink.

"Do you believe that He can save you, if you'll trust Him?"

Another blink.

"Reno, I'm going to pray for you, and then I want you to pray and tell the Lord you know you're a sinner and ask Him to save you. Will you do that?"

He blinked again.

I prayed for him for a long time, then waited for him to pray. He lay there with his eyes closed for several minutes, then opened his eyes and looked at me with a faint smile. "Did you pray?" I asked.

He blinked his eyes once.

"Did you mean it?"

He blinked again.

"Reno, if you meant it, I want you to listen to this verse." I read to him John 5:24, "Verily, verily, I say unto you, He that heareth my word, and believeth on him that sent me, hath everlasting life, and shall not come into condemnation; but is passed from death unto life."

"If you've truly trusted Christ, that's what's happened to you Reno; and though your body may die, your soul will live in heaven forever." The man closed his eyes, and I spoke softly. "I'll see you in heaven."

That was the last time I saw him alive. Reno died before I could return to Charleston for another visit.

Chapter
Twenty-Five

For I am persuaded, that neither death, nor life, nor angels, nor principalities, nor powers, nor things present, nor things to come, nor height, nor depth, nor any other creature, shall be able to separate us from the love of God, which is in Christ Jesus our Lord.

Romans 8:38–39

Just a few days before Christmas Brenda came home, but we had no house. With winter coming on and the money exhausted, plus the new responsibilities of caring for Brenda, I could not get the house ready for quite a while.

* * *

The children were having problems. They had been shuffled around for months. Although everyone was kind and good to them, they were feeling the strain of not having their own parents. They fought a lot between themselves and with the McCandlesses' children. We knew we needed a place of our own. But first there was Christmas to consider, and I couldn't wait to see Becky.

* * *

The parents of my volunteer assistant pastor had moved out west for a temporary job. He planned to move into their apartment and we would move into his mobile home. Debbie and Johnny would share a small bedroom. At last Brenda and I would be able to start putting our family back together.

The dressing changes were down to an hour in the morning and an hour in the evening. Brenda was wearing the Jobst pressure garments from head to toe. Like an extremely tight girdle, tailor-made for the person wearing them, these tan elastic garments were fastened with Velcro and extremely difficult to get off and on. Brenda wore a face mask, long-sleeved vest, gloves, and stockings down to her toes. We were glad it was winter.

Our prayer was that Brenda would be strong enough to travel to Cincinnati to see Becky for Christmas. Sometime in December Becky had started to respond. She would sit up and often try to eat baby food. The nurses had sent more pictures. She looked rough. There was tremendous swelling in her body. One of her front teeth had been broken out when she had thrashed during a bronchoscopy, a procedure in which they inserted a large tube down her trachea to examine the burn scars from inhaling the flames. I shared these pictures with Brenda because I wanted to prepare her for what lay ahead.

On Christmas Eve, we started north. Brenda's father and stepmother still lived in Corbin, Kentucky, five hours away. It took us nearly ten hours to get there. The frequent stops and adjustments, and moving around trying to help Brenda get comfortable slowed us down considerably. When we arrived in Corbin, Brenda was determined to find a gift for Becky. She wanted to buy a stuffed animal with a music box inside. We looked everywhere, but could only find a teddy bear costing $65. We couldn't afford it, and Brenda cried. Thankfully, Kathy Martin, Dr. Bob Jones' secretary, had sent gifts for our entire family from BJU. Whatever was in the little box for Becky would have to do.

We spent Christmas morning with Brenda's folks and then took nearly six hours to make the three-hour trip to Cincinnati. We arrived Christmas evening, just after dark. The head nurse had returned to the hospital to be with Becky when we arrived. My brother had left his family at home, gone over and dressed in surgical clothes to wait beside Becky's bed until we got there. A young doctor from India doing his internship at the Shriners Burns Hospital had bought Becky a little red dress. One of the nurses had tied a red ribbon in the only little tuft of hair she had left above her forehead.

Before going into the Intensive Care Unit, we talked with the doctor and nurse outside, who briefed Brenda as much as possible on what to expect. Becky had a trach tube in her throat and an IV in her head. Her arms and legs were bandaged with Ace Wraps to keep pressure on the scars. One of her eyelids was badly contracted and the eye was not really open. Her left arm was very stiff; it wouldn't bend at the elbow, and the hand was turned back at ninety degrees to the arm.

"Mrs. Vaughn," the nurse began, "we're not sure if she's going to know you—either of you," she said as she looked at me. "She is awake, but we don't know how much she understands. Her heart has stopped many times. It's too early to tell if there has been any brain damage."

Brenda removed her Jobst mask and fashioned the wig she was wearing to look as much like her natural hair as possible. Her face was still very red from the new scars, and she was tired and haggard-looking from the trip. Debbie and Johnny clung to my arms. We made the walk down the long hallway, pushing Brenda in the wheelchair. Then we turned a corner and walked down another long hallway to the windows of the Intensive Care Unit. I felt like a condemned man on his way to his execution.

Becky had been wrenched from Brenda's arms in flames, then swept away to a hospital in a distant city seven months and five days ago. So much had happened—surgery again and again. Brenda's hospital bill had totaled over $175,000. Our family had been torn apart and would never be the same again. Though no longer in critical condition, Becky was still in intensive care. Having barely survived herself, Brenda now had to face the reality of Becky's appearance and helplessness.

We finally stopped just outside the window. Everything was silent. I saw a doctor. *Or is it? No, it's Harold!*

I looked at my brother, and he looked back at me with the same look that nurse had given me that night in May in the emergency room. I glanced at the nurse and then my wife. Volumes were spoken by all, but only with our eyes. Anticipation hung in the air, thick and heavy.

I nodded to the nurse. She turned, picked Becky up and carried her over to the window. Harold, a young doctor, and another nurse gathered behind her. Brenda, Debbie, Johnny, and I bunched together, our faces pressed up to the glass, our arms around each other. Becky was actually in front of us, in the nurse's arms.

Becky looked first at me and then at Brenda. As she stared into her mother's eyes, she began to breathe very deeply and rapidly. Her mouth opened into a big, broken-toothed smile as tears streamed down her cheeks.

All of us were crying. Neither Brenda nor Becky saw the scars; they only saw each other.

* * *

Within an hour we were dressed to enter the ICU. We cautiously approached Becky's crib. All day I had prayed, *Lord, I have to have something to help me. I'm afraid I can't handle this, and I must be strong for Becky.*

Not until I actually held Becky in my arms did that "something" come. As I sat down in a rocking chair, John laid her in my arms. I looked into her eyes, and the Scripture came to mind, "Man looketh on the outward appearance, but God looketh on the heart."

I thought of those friends who had passed out when they first saw me in Charleston. At the time, I had not understood. I hadn't known what I looked like. I didn't feel ugly or frightening inside. I realized Becky didn't know how she looked. She was the same little girl I had loved and enjoyed so much. Only the outside had changed—Becky was the same. And now, she needed me more than ever.

The time came to open Becky's present. I struggled with my weakened, gloved hands to open the box from Bob Jones University—the only present we had for her.

It was a little, blue, stuffed donkey with a wind-up key on the bottom. With a few turns of the key, the donkey's head began to sway gently and the melodious strains of the "Donkey Serenade" softly filled the room.

The nurse had warned us, "she shows no interest in life, she's far too withdrawn." I offered the little toy to Becky, and we held our breath. Becky slowly reached toward it and with her awkward little hand began to stroke its back. Tears of joy flowed as we watched the smile on her face.

Part Four

The Fine Gold

But he knoweth the way that I take: when he hath tried me, I shall come forth as gold.

Job 23:10

Chapter
Twenty-Six

Wherefore seeing we also are compassed about with so great a cloud of witnesses, let us lay aside every weight, and the sin which doth so easily beset us, and let us run with patience the race that is set before us.

Hebrews 12:1

Brenda's determination was added to mine. Becky would make it. We would do whatever we could to help her. We didn't realize then how little we would be able to do for her because there was still so much to do for each other.

Brenda wanted to be with Becky all the time, but she was still practically helpless herself. Not only did she have the lengthy and painful dressing changes to undergo every day, but she, like everyone else, was required to change from street clothes into surgical scrub clothes in order to visit Becky. Going through that twice a day completely exhausted her.

But Becky was responding. She started taking solid food and allowed Brenda to feed her. Brenda tired very quickly and spent most of the time just sitting by Becky's bed. Although Becky made regular eye contact, only one eye seemed to focus. From time to time she smiled, and she was always glad to see us. After a week the doctors and nurses set up a filming session one morning to film our arrival. The film would document the value of parents' support in a child's recovery. Becky's nurse, Terri, was writing an article about Becky's survival for a nursing journal. The dramatic change in Becky's behavior and recovery when both her parents were with her was one of the key points.

Becky still had the trach tube in her throat; and although no longer on oxygen, she was not breathing normally. Occasionally, the respiratory therapist would help her with her breathing. One afternoon, Brenda and I were in the room alone with Becky. The nurse had stepped out for just a moment. I was talking to Becky, who was watching me closely. She looked as if she was trying to respond.

"Honey, I think she's trying to talk to us!" I said excitedly. I knew she couldn't speak with the trach tube in her throat, but she was moving her lips.

I said, "Becky, are you trying to talk to me?" She smiled with her little broken-toothed smile.

We didn't know if Becky could talk at all. There was scarring in her throat, and she hadn't spoken for nearly eight months. Although she once had the vocabulary of a bright two-year-old, she had surely lost most of her ability to speak through lack of use.

Slowly, I put my forefinger over the plastic tube that opened into her neck and said, "Becky, say 'Daddy.' " Just as I had coached her before she was a year old, I urged her on. "Come on, Becky, say 'Daddy,' say 'Daddy' for me."

Her mouth formed the words. At first, she whispered it, "Daddy," and then stronger, a louder whisper, as I urged her on. Finally, in a hoarse voice that was obviously hers, she pronounced it: a clear but faint, "Daddy." Brenda and I both cried. Becky cried with us.

The nurse sauntered back in and wondered what was going on. "Why is everyone crying?" she asked.

"Becky's talking!" I announced.

"Becky, are you talking?" the nurse asked.

Becky smiled through her tears. Without asking for permission, I showed the nurse what Becky could do, and the nurse cried with us.

* * *

With our home gone and our family scattered among friends and relatives for so long, I had come to depend on our reunion more than I realized. I had not seen our new house yet, and so many of our possessions—

the little things that help us hold our lives together—had either been destroyed or placed in storage. All I wanted was to hold Becky, to sing to her, and tell her stories, to live for those few minutes of pleasure that punctuated the long hours of boredom and pain.

But we had to go home. Debbie and Johnny needed the stability of regular meals and familiar beds, even if they were borrowed. John and I both dreaded the day we would have to leave for South Carolina. The hospital in Charleston had saved my life, but I didn't care if I ever saw it again. I almost resented the fact we were obligated to live so far away, but our lives were there, and our hope and help were there.

Leaving Becky back in May was not a choice I had been allowed to make; leaving her now was not a choice either. God had taught me that trying to delay His will is a futile substitute for really having control. John assured me he would visit Becky regularly until I could come again. We would have to leave her with the Lord in Cincinnati.

* * *

As we moved into the first week of January, it was getting harder and harder for Brenda to go to the hospital. She tired quickly. We were both physically and emotionally exhausted. Becky experienced a few bad days to balance off the good days. We could stay no longer.

When the day finally came to leave, we had no way to explain to Becky. She had lived in the hospital longer than she could remember. In many ways she knew the nurses better than she knew us. But they knew what was best for her. Her physical needs were great, and we couldn't meet them. Now we had to get home where Brenda could get well.

With lots of promises that we'd come back, we left Becky staring blankly at the ceiling and cried our way down I-75. We called every day, the nurses gave us reports, and my brother visited Becky regularly, but we simply had to concentrate on Brenda's needs. Each day Brenda's dressing changes became easier. Her open wounds were healing, and her strength was slowly returning. Brenda's joints were so stiff she couldn't get out of bed by herself, but slowly she began to get involved in the duties of the home.

We were still staying in my assistant pastor's trailer. Brenda tried her best to help with the meals and the dishes. One afternoon she was in the kitchen washing a few dishes from lunch, when she cried out for me to come quickly. Thinking that she had been hurt, I bolted into the kitchen. Brenda was fine. While washing a cup, she had suddenly realized that she was able to rotate her wrist. Almost in disbelief, she showed me how she could turn her hand, palm up and then palm down. Such a little thing, really, and yet a major victory. We both understood that for Brenda, the road to recovery was going to be easier now. For her, the worst was behind.

There would be little improvements every day. We were learning to laugh and have fun again as a family. One morning while helping Brenda get into the Jobst garments that she wore from head to toe—they were tan colored and literally covered her body: face mask, gloves, long-sleeved vest, and stockings—I said to her, "You look like an ant."

"Thanks a lot," she replied.

"No, really, I mean it. Take a look at this." I picked up two pencils from the desk in the bedroom and held them to her head like antennae. We both laughed until we cried.

But the biggest laugh was the day she "pulled a robbery at Pizza City." Because we didn't want to cook, one of the men in the church and I had eaten regularly at a restaurant called Pizza City while remodeling the house. We had started a Bible study with the fellows there after work and had led several of them to the Lord. None of them had ever seen Brenda.

I took her there one night for pizza. The man behind the counter was tossing his pizza dough into the air as we walked through the door. Although Brenda wore a wig over her Jobst mask, the poor fellow froze in fear. The dough dropped over his arms, and he stared at her.

"It's okay," I assured him. "She was badly burned. Really, it's okay."

With a look of relief, he leaned across the counter to support himself and announced in a thick Italian accent, "I thought she gonna rob me."

On Brenda's first trip to the grocery store, we met the fellow whose house I had visited on the night of the fire. He took one look at Brenda and his knees buckled. I helped him sit down in the aisle and Brenda watched over him, telling him to put his head between his knees. I ran to the refrigerator case to retrieve a jar of orange juice, opened it, and gave it to him to drink right there in the aisle.

"Boy, I'm really embarrassed," he declared.

On our way home, we laughed, wondering if he had even liked orange juice, and what he had said to the cashier when he tried to pay for the open jar.

That night, Brenda made a statement that gave me a glimpse of how God was going to use her in the years ahead. She said, "Honey, it's going to be up to me to help others with this. I've come to accept it and I know you have, but I can't expect other people to understand or to know how to respond. I'm going to have to take the initiative and teach Becky to do the same. We've got to find a way to honor the Lord with this thing."

The conversation opened up a more personal matter between us. I had been trying my best to be as careful and gentle with Brenda as possible. I tried to show her as much tenderness and affection as possible, but I was afraid of hurting her. She told me that she felt like I was rejecting her, and she didn't blame me if her appearance was offensive to me. We knew we would get through the difficulty of resuming our normal physical relationship somehow; we had done so twice before, after lengthy military separation. But this was different. I had not anticipated Brenda's fear of being ugly. She was not unattractive to me. Without going into detail or being indiscreet, and to answer the inevitable questions this brings up, we can share that this was one of the easier hurdles we had to overcome.

A few months later, Brenda was speaking at the Bill Rice Ranch. Our fourth child was obviously on the way. She knew what the hundreds of ladies were thinking as she shared the testimony of her injuries. "I guess I'm sort of like that old teapot you ladies have on your stove at home," she stated. "It might not look like much, but it works!"

When I heard that on tape, I blushed, but I joined the laughter that lasted for nearly a minute.

But that winter, before Becky came home, there wasn't much to laugh about. One night we got a call from Cincinnati. It was the head nurse. "Reverend Vaughn," she said, "I'm concerned about Becky. Physically, she's improving, but I think she's depressed. She doesn't

want to eat, and she won't respond to us. I think her heart is broken that you left."

"What can we do?" I asked.

"I don't know," she answered, "but if she's going to make it, she's
going to have to be with you and Mrs. Vaughn."

Chapter
Twenty-Seven

Looking unto Jesus, the author and finisher of our faith; who for the joy that was set before him endured the cross, despising the shame, and is set down at the right hand of the throne of God.

Hebrews 12:2

We knew that we could not take care of Becky. Her physical needs for bandaging, therapy, and even the continued use of intravenous fluids made it impossible for us to bring her home. Brenda couldn't lift her, and in order to make ends meet I was still working at UPS and at other odd jobs to supplement my income from the church. Debbie and Johnny were back in school and were too young to help with Becky when they were at home in the evening. We knew that Becky would come home sooner or later. I had to get the house done, but progress on the renovation had virtually stopped. Bad weather and lack of time put us at a standstill, even when we had a few dollars to buy more materials. What I had hoped would take only a few weeks had already taken months; and at the rate I was going, it would be several more months before we could move in. Our resources were exhausted, and our strength was gone. We had some of the toughest decisions yet to make. We needed some miracles.

Since the Shriners hospital in Greenville is an orthopedic hospital, it is not equipped to care for acute burn patients. Initially, we had ruled it out, but now as Brenda and I were praying for some options, it occurred to both of us that maybe the Shriners hospital could take care of Becky. This way we could be with her until she got through the present crisis.

Since we knew Terri better than any of the other nurses, I called her and suggested the Greenville unit. "Let me check into it," she responded.

Within a week we were making plans to have Becky transferred to Greenville. A small airplane would take me to Cincinnati where I would pick Becky up and bring her home.

It doesn't snow much in South Carolina, but that January it did. Twice the trip had to be canceled because of bad weather. It was mid-February before we could make the flight. Even then the weather was bad. It was foggy in Cincinnati, and the runways were icy. But a kind man named Garrett flew the little twin-engine plane beautifully, breaking through the low clouds at Cincinnati's Lunken Airport, side-slipping the plane down onto the runway, and carefully maneuvering over the ice. A Shriners van met us.

We were at the hospital in a matter of minutes. Mounds of dirty snow on the sides of the road clogged the traffic. The jingle of tire chains clattered around us rhythmically as we pulled into the hospital complex in the Avondale community where half a dozen hospitals sit clustered on a hill above the University of Cincinnati. This had been Becky's home for nearly a year, and she had never seen it. Today she would.

Becky was in a wheelchair in the hallway of the third floor and ready to go when I arrived. Terri accompanied her. She was coming to Greenville with us. Becky was wrapped tightly with Ace Wraps under a little knit suit. Ann, Becky's other nurse, had bought her a pretty pink and blue scarf, almost as large as a blanket. A matching knit cap was pulled down around the little stubs of her ears. As I walked down the hallway to meet her, Becky beamed a big smile. There were hugs and kisses and lots of excitement. Becky obviously knew what we were doing. She was eager to go.

"Aren't there papers to sign?" I asked as we walked toward the elevator.

"No," Terri answered, "I'll take care of all of that. I understand the weather's getting worse; we've got to leave right away."

"Okay with me," I chimed in. "How about you, Becky?" She turned her head and didn't take her eyes off me.

Other nurses, some doctors, the dietician, several orderlies, and a number of the ambulatory patients had formed a little crowd near the ambulance entrance downstairs. The ambulance was ready, and as the EMS technicians lifted Becky from the wheelchair and strapped her into the ambulance, her friends cheered her on. The young lady who sat in the back with Becky asked if I would like to ride with her.

"Sure," I said, and I buckled in beside her. Becky watched me with a big smile. Several times the traffic noises and the movement of the van frightened her. I comforted her by talking softly to her and telling her about Mommy, Debbie, and Johnny.

Soon Becky was asleep. The plane ride home was bumpy, and we were in clouds most of the time. I was thankful Terri was with Becky. As we touched down and taxied into the Greenville downtown airport, I looked out the window. The weather was better here with very little snow on the ground. Then, I noticed a crowd of people near the gate. Cameras had been set up everywhere. Signs poked up above the crowd: "Welcome Home, Becky" and "To God Be the Glory." Several Shriners stood there, wearing their fez hats. People from the newspaper and from Channel 4 TV waited as well.

What a grand reunion we had! There were hugs and kisses and shouts of joy. As I approached the gate with my little girl in my arms, I realized that most of my congregation were there, too. And they were singing "To God Be the Glory."

* * *

A dear lady named Betty from our church had become almost a full-time nurse to me. With her help I was able to join the group from our church and go to the airport. A large turnout of our friends made everything wonderful. Johnny perched on the shoulders of one of the men while Debbie pressed her face against the fence. After the plane stopped in front of us, John walked down the steps with Becky in his arms and headed straight toward us. I'll never forget the joy I felt as we sang and praised God for His goodness. I held Becky in my arms as we drove to the local Shriners hospital. Her smile had returned, and I was getting stronger. I knew then we would make it.

* * *

While Brenda waited to hold Becky, the news media interviewed me briefly. That evening Becky's homecoming appeared on the six o'clock news. The testimony of our faith in the Lord and the singing of our people brought a blessing to tens of thousands who had prayed for that day. From the airport, we took Becky straight to the Greenville unit of the Shriners hospitals and got her admitted. Terri stayed with Becky for several days until she got acquainted with the nurses and felt comfortable. She wouldn't need any more surgery for a while. She just needed the close care of the nurses and lots of therapy.

With the help of the ladies in the church, Brenda was able to spend quite a bit of time with Becky, and her improvement was remarkable. Although dozens of people helped us, there were two without whom we couldn't have made it. Kathy became Becky's "Aunt Kathy," and Betty became a part of our family.

At last, I was going to be able to give more attention to remodeling the house; now all we needed was the money.

Chapter
Twenty-Eight

For consider him that endured such contradiction of sinners against himself, lest ye be wearied and faint in your minds. Ye have not yet resisted unto blood, striving against sin.

Hebrews 12:3–4

Debbie and Johnny were able to visit Becky in the Greenville hospital. It encouraged her greatly to see them regularly, and it helped them too. Johnny had such a tender heart. It was very hard for him to see her in pain and suffering. One day after Johnny had been to the hospital, we were sitting around the supper table. I knew something was on his mind.

"What are you thinking about, buddy?" I asked.

"Dad, are they going to make Becky some new ears?"

"Well, maybe. There are lots of things they can do to help her. She still needs a lot of surgery. I'm not sure what they'll do, but maybe."

He looked disappointed.

"Probably," I added.

"If they make her new ears, will she be able to hear?"

Bless his heart! I had assumed the children knew everything I knew—that they understood—but until now Johnny and Debbie had seen Becky only through the window at Shriners on two or three occasions. They had not been with her over those months. They didn't know what all this meant. I explained that Becky could already hear, that she couldn't talk much because of the trach tube, and that she had probably forgotten how to talk.

"She can hear what you say, though, Johnny," I assured him, "and I know she wants to hear anything you want to tell her."

He smiled and seemed reassured. At eight years old, Johnny had experienced too much pain for one little boy's lifetime: separated from his father for nearly two years; major surgery himself; and now all this turmoil in his life. It had taken its toll on him. He is a strong man today, but we grieved for years over the price he and Debbie paid during this time.

The Shriners hospital in Greenville was well-staffed and the people were nice, but the building was nearly fifty years old. However, Becky continued to improve. With Brenda home and Becky nearby, I put my extra time into working on the house.

Miraculously, day by day, the Lord provided for the materials. My good friend, Bernie, who had been with me often since the night of the fire, helped me every day that I could work on the house. We still laugh about the time we nailed down the last sheet of plywood on the upstairs floor. We looked around to admire our work, only to realize we had not put in a stairway! Dan had to send the saw up through the window so we could cut our way out.

While looking for a house to purchase near the church, I had been able to obtain a small house for the church behind our auditorium building. We were then able to purchase three more homes in the same block. We would later remodel these to use for Sunday school rooms and offices, since we were running out of Sunday school space. Because I owned the house across the street from the church, I made it available for classes until we moved into it. We held Sunday school there even with the open stud walls. On Saturday evenings we swept up the sawdust and set up chairs for Sunday. In the year since the fire our congregation had grown to over two hundred. Although my assistant was still a volunteer, I was finally full-time. Soon my assistant would need his trailer again. But the house still wasn't ready! We prayed.

One afternoon I received a call from a member of our former church. He and some friends had purchased a community of small houses that they were remodeling for students at Furman University. He wanted us to have one of his two-bedroom houses for as long as we needed it, at no charge. We lived there from April to July.

There was never enough time to do what needed to be done: work on the house, work with the church, preaching, counseling, visiting. Brenda still needed a great deal of care. We visited Becky every day, often several times a day. I didn't know what to neglect and what to try to get done.

Tom Harper had visited us and given me a set of cassette tapes containing six sermons by Dr. Charles Stanley of the First Baptist Church in Atlanta. The title of the series was "Brokenness." I listened to the entire series more than twenty times. While I was working on the house, I would often stop, sit down on a paint bucket with my head in my hands, and listen. The Bible principles helped me make sense of everything that had happened in the previous year.

Of course, I thought. *That's what it's all about!*

We had learned many valuable lessons. Many verses of Scripture had come alive to Brenda and me during the many months in the hospital and my tens of thousands of miles on the highway. We knew God loved us. We knew that He might, in some way, even be chastening us. He was certainly purging the dross from our lives. But I had never heard, nor understood, the concept of brokenness: that God does not always send pain into our lives to punish, but sometimes to perfect. The fiery trial began to make sense. The smelting process, though not enjoyed, was beginning to be appreciated.

In the following year, I adapted those principles into a series of messages on brokenness for my own church. Through those messages, God sent revival. Souls were saved, Christians were challenged, and the church grew. We were running out of room.

Feverishly, I worked to finish the house. In June, when Becky had to return to Cincinnati for surgery and a brief follow-up treatment, Brenda was strong enough to go with her. I threw all my energies into getting the house finished. Becky returned to Greenville late in July, but not to the hospital. This time, she came home!

Chapter
Twenty-Nine

And ye have forgotten the exhortation which speaketh unto you as unto children, My son, despise not thou the chastening of the Lord, nor faint when thou art rebuked of him: For whom the Lord loveth he chasteneth, and scourgeth every son whom he receiveth.

Hebrews 12:5–6

JULY 29, 1979

Our family started over. At last we were together again. Somehow that day marked a return to a normal life. Yet in spite of the pain, and the surgery, and the many times we thought Becky surely would die, the year ahead proved to be one of the most difficult of our lives.

The financial pressure was unbelievable. With church membership nearing three hundred, people couldn't even get into the building. We installed speakers on the outside of the building, and people sat on cars in the parking lot. We knew we had to do something.

There was no way that we could get into a building program. The church congregation was too young. I was too immature in my leadership. It would be too big a responsibility for any of us to face at that time.

In August, Bernie, Dan, my assistant pastor, and I drove to Texas to attend the advanced Bill Gothard seminar in Denton. It was a life-changing experience. The principles I learned and the truths pre-

198

sented held new meaning for me since the fire. My message was being crystallized. Brenda and I were learning what it meant to be broken. We were learning what it meant to be transparent, learning to reveal even those painful things about ourselves that were necessary to help others.

Later that year, I attended a week-long seminar for pastors in Bloomington, Indiana, also sponsored by the Institute in Basic Youth Conflicts. Dr. Stanley was there. One day I had the opportunity to sit down with him at lunch. I related to him how much his "Brokenness" series had helped me, and I briefly told him about Brenda and Becky.

"Someone asked prayer for you," he said. "We've prayed for you. How is your family?"

I told him how they were doing and how God had blessed our church. I also mentioned the dilemma we were facing in running out of room. "I've been praying about multiple services. What do you think about that idea?" I asked.

"Well," he replied, "it's possible, but it's very tiring. You'll wear yourself and your people out, but it is a good short-term solution."

When I got home, I shared the idea with some other pastor friends, some of my former professors at Bob Jones, and the men in our church. Multiple services seemed like the solution to our problems. Late that year, we implemented a new schedule: the first service was at 8:30 on Sunday mornings, then Sunday school, then the 11 A.M. service. We started with two evening services. In the spring, we expanded it to three: one at 4:30, one at 6:00, and one at 7:30. For the next two years, I preached five times each Sunday. The church grew to eight hundred.

During this time, Becky had to return to Cincinnati about once a month. She would stay for several days. Women from the church would often take Brenda and Becky on these trips. In the fall of 1979, Brenda and Becky were invited to the Bill Rice Ranch near Murfreesboro, Tennessee. The Bill Rice Ranch is a summer camp with a year-round program for the deaf. Dr. and Mrs. Bill Rice had started it after having had a deaf daughter themselves years before. Brenda spoke to the ladies about the fire and the lessons we were learning about brokenness. She talked with them about transparency, about the burden we felt for others who had to go through what we were going through without the Lord, about how God was touching our hearts for the needs of other handicapped children like Becky, children who often have no parents to love them and no church in which to grow. In a message that has since been shared with thousands by tape, and with millions on Dr. James Dobson's *Focus on the Family* radio broadcast, Brenda offered the first key to how the Lord was leading us to share what we were discovering: that there is something in life more precious than gold.

* * *

Although I was content to let John speak for the family, invitations began to come in from all over the country for me to share my testimony. I thought back to a time shortly after coming to Faith Baptist Church. I was mopping the floor one day when a realization struck me: *Pastors' wives have to speak to ladies' groups! Lord, please don't ever make me do that! I couldn't!*

But I needed to share what God was teaching me. People could be helped by it. Others had prayed for us and truly wanted to know the whole story. My first meeting was a linen shower held by Mrs. Handford to restore all the linens we had lost. To my surprise, when my turn came to speak, I found that I wasn't tongue-tied. In fact, I found it difficult to stop because I had so much to share about what God had done for me.

The invitations increased. Often people asked for Becky and me to come together. I realized that God had given us a tremendous opportunity to present the lessons He'd given us: "You can't always control your circumstances, but you can control your response. . . . He will give you the strength you need to face the circumstances. . . . Some things may never work out in this life, but God has promised that when we get to heaven all things will have *worked together for good.* The verse doesn't say that all things are good. We live in a world where bad things happen, and people do evil. We're human, and we make mistakes. And we suffer for them. But I look forward to God showing me how all these things are working together for His goal of Christlikeness for each of us."

Sometimes still, as I watch Becky struggle, I pray that God will strengthen her. I pray that she will have a vision for a ministry of her own. If Becky were to die today, she would have reached more people for the Lord by her testimony than I ever will in my lifetime. I can imagine the Lord welcoming her to heaven, "Well done, Becky. Welcome home." For eternity she will have a new body. She'll know the joy and the reward she has earned serving God in this life.

* * *

As our ministry broadened and our understanding deepened, by the grace of God the bills were being paid, but the deeper debts were mounting. We knew we were accountable for the lessons we were learning. There is no way to repay all the help we received, except through a renewed dedication to make our lives count for God. We closed as many accounts as we could, picked up the rest of our things from Tom's garage, and brought our little dog, Bob, home to the new house. The church encouraged me to hire a secretary and some assistant pastors to keep up with the ministry. I was able to get my correspondence out and thank the many people who had helped us for so long. God was clearly impressing on our hearts, however, that our greatest debt was not to those who had helped us, but to those who needed our help.

The financial help from the insurance at UPS is a testimony to the value that organization places on its personnel. We will rejoice if this book is an encouragement to the people at UPS.

The debt we owe to the Shriners is even deeper. Some may wonder why we were ever concerned about taking help from them. Others may think we were wrong to do so. I must admit that my hesitation at first was not because I felt I would compromise principles, but because I feared others would think so. When I learned that the Shriners hospitals were the place where Becky could get the best medical care possible, the decision was made. As a father, that was my obligation to her.

The good works done by the Shriners are truly good. We can never thank them enough. I have written letters to the editor of our local paper to defend them, spoken at their banquets to express appreciation, and yes, accepted hundreds of thousands of dollars in medical assistance from them. We know many Shriners personally as friends. We are deeply indebted and thankful for their help.

From this perspective, let me kindly speak to any Shriners who may be reading this story. If your good works are done to honor the Lord Jesus Christ, whom you have trusted as personal Savior, then you can expect eternal rewards. But if you hope to offer good works to God as the purchase price of eternal life, you will miss it. Salvation is not earned by the efforts of man—it is the gift of God, purchased for us by the blood of Jesus Christ alone. I know that many of you are sincerely striving to serve God, but others are still seeking Him. God is to be found in Christ Himself, not simply in Christ's example. We would not truly show our gratitude to you if we were too timid to tell you this.

And it would be unchristian for us to leave this subject without appealing to our friends who have questions about the Shriners. The Shriners burns hospitals are an example of genuine compassion—they are among the finest medical institutions in existence. It grieves us to hear glib and careless statements, often judgmental, about others who are genuinely sincere. These statements do not demonstrate Christ's compassion to others, who are often more compassionate than we ourselves. If we are debtors at all, we are indebted first to the truth.

Chapter Thirty

If ye endure chastening, God dealeth with you as with sons; for what son is he whom the father chasteneth not? But if ye be without chastisement, whereof all are partakers, then are ye bastards, and not sons.

Hebrews 12:7–8

My physical appearance and limitations have improved through the years of therapy and reconstructive surgery. Actually, my appearance has never been a problem for me or for John—at least he has never given me any indication that it has. Oh sure, I was concerned at first, but he has always been completely accepting and understanding. For several years I wore long sleeves and tight collars, but I have become more and more content just to relax and use the reactions of others as opportunities to share my testimony.

When Joey, our fifth child, was a baby, people would think the scars on my neck were wrinkles. They complimented me on my "grandbaby." I sometimes explained that he was my own baby until one dear soul blurted out, "You're kidding!" After that I'd just smile and say, "Yes, he's pretty grand."

My acceptance of the scars is easy because John accepts them. There are long periods of time, days and weeks, when I don't see Becky's scars—I see Becky. I know that's how John sees me. We're like two people who continue to love each other as they grow old and wrinkled together. I just got there first!

* * *

The year after the fire was a rude awakening. We were in over our heads. The church had outgrown our ability to lead it. We had a large ministry, but its management was a nightmare. I felt the way Moses must have felt. I had been on the back side of the desert, but here I was in the wilderness with a mob I didn't know how to help. My wife was weak, my daughter was permanently handicapped, and my two older children had been neglected for over a year. Although I had preached it and would have said before that I believed it, I was just beginning to understand what it means to be totally dependent on the Lord.

The pain was relieved, the traveling was reduced, but so were many of the benefits. People facing tragedy receive a lot of attention—emotional and moral support from others—but people in the daily grind often struggle alone.

However, new people were coming into our lives all the time—people who knew us but whom we didn't know, people who often assumed we were superhuman. We met people who thought that we had survived the fire, kept our family together, and seen the growth of our ministry not because of the grace of God that is available to everyone, but somehow because we were different. It was flattering and it appealed to our pride, but we knew better.

Over and over again we saw two common ideas as God gave us opportunities to minister to others. One was the mistaken notion that somehow we had earned a guarantee from God that we would never again have a tough time. Our suffering was behind us. Our pain was over. We had made it through. We were special. We were the exception. Of course, that's self-centered; it's worldly, carnal, wicked thinking at its worst, and naiveté at its best.

The other idea was that, because Becky was handicapped, she was now in a very special class of people who were allowed to live by a different set of rules. Because of her suffering, in some strange way she had an edge on everyone else. Society had to give her a break. She had experienced her brush with death and had had the last laugh—now she deserved special treatment. We saw this attitude generally held, even by Christian people, toward the handicapped. Our hearts were increasingly burdened to help Becky realize that, although she was special and would not enjoy in this life many of the things others enjoy, she, unlike many others, had no choice—she *had* to live her life in the context of eternity.

Our family, and especially Becky, attracted attention everywhere we went. People would stop and speak and sometimes be encouraging; others would stare. Some were downright offensive. For nearly two years, we had taken strength from the positive attention, but we knew we couldn't continue to attract that kind of attention to ourselves. Through this, however, we recognized a new opportunity—an opportunity to tell others the truth we were learning: that God's grace is sufficient . . . that He is not a shelter from the storm, but a shelter in the storm . . . that the fiery trial is not alien to the Christian life, but basic.

The more we faced this opportunity, the more it became an obligation. We had to find a way to teach Becky a truth that no unbeliever acknowledges and few Christians have realized: A handicap is a responsibility! It is an exclamation point in a person's life message. Whatever we're saying with our lives, we say more emphatically if we are disabled. If we're living for self, for material things, for the trinkets of the world, it's going to be obvious.

What could be more absurd than a beauty pageant for the burned? But if we're living for the Lord, if God's grace is real in our lives, the "beauty" of a handicap is an undeniably powerful testimony by which even the devil is confounded.

"No wonder Job serves you," Satan challenged the Lord. "Look how you've blessed him."

But when Job proclaimed, "though he slay me, yet will I trust him," his critics had only empty arguments.

In the years that followed, many precious things were done for Becky: special outings, horseback rides, picnics, trips to Disney World. All of these brought laughter and joy into a young life that has known more pain than most will ever know. But we knew the day would come when Becky would be a teenager, when she would look into the mirror and see that she, truly, was different. We had to find a way to help her know God's definition of beauty and to reject the world's.

During that painful year after Becky came home, we realized that although Brenda and Becky did look different, in fact all of us were different. Another milestone came when we attended a revival at

Hampton Park Baptist Church where Dr. Bill Rice III, the son of the man who had founded the camp for the deaf, was preaching.

* * *

At the revival meeting I reached a new understanding of the events God had permitted in our lives. I told the Lord, "I am thankful for what You allowed my family to experience." Because He showed me then just a little taste of what hell would be like and what I would never have to suffer for eternity, the Lord gave me a whole new appreciation for my salvation. For the first time I could truly say that, if I could go back to May 20, 1978, and change it, I would not. I am today what God has helped me to be because of the things He helped me through.

That night I went down the aisle at the invitation just as I had done when John preached on the Fiery Trial. I hesitated this time, not because I was reluctant to be transparent with God, but because I knew we were attracting so much attention. Even now, our prayer is that this experience will attract attention not to us, but to the Lord. He is the One who deserves all the glory.

For Becky's sake, I still struggle, and I know she does, too. But she is coming to that same place in her life. I still pray that God will give her a vision for her ministry and help her see the one she's already had. Sometimes in my flesh I feel sorry for her, but then I remind myself of the day ahead when we will come before the Lord. Becky will stand with the thousands of people she has influenced; I will stand with the few I have influenced. I wonder whom I will feel sorry for then? It will all be clear. Then we will know true thankfulness.

* * *

And Brenda truly is thankful. I have often heard her say to others, "How glad I am that I can understand Becky's needs. What a blessing it is that God allowed me to go through what Becky went through." She speaks about how she knew God's hand was on Becky's life, how the Lord helped her help Becky understand. What neither of us realized then, and what Brenda still can hardly believe, is how God is using Brenda not just to help Becky with a ministry, but to have a ministry of her own.

The wisdom God has given Brenda was expressed succinctly one day in a response she gave to Becky. On the testimony of this simple statement, we have built a ministry, and thousands of lives have been changed. Becky was trying to look through a picture book. For about ten minutes she had been trying to turn the page with her little, fingerless hands. Debbie was playing the piano. As Brenda worked in the kitchen, Becky asked, "Mommy, when I grow up, will I have hands like Debbie?"

As I read quietly in the next room, I listened to hear her response.

Brenda stopped her work and said softly, "Becky, Debbie has the hands that God has given her to do her job, and you have the hands that God has allowed you to have to do your job."

Out of that simple statement has grown the "Hidden Treasure" principle, a central theme of our ministry, especially our ministry with disabled children: "We have everything we need to do the will of God for our lives."

And in so many ways, Becky has so much more. God has used her countless times to show His love for me. I clearly remember a particular day I had stopped by the hospital to see her. She was asleep. I looked at her hands—twisted and scarred, little stubs where her fingers had been. And I thought about the day that she had stuck her fingers through the backstop at the park and how I had called "time out" from the game while she puckered her little lips through the fence to give me a kiss.

She has the hands she needs to do her job, I thought. I knew it was true, but I wondered what it meant. *What is her job? How will God use this little girl?*

As I stood beside her bed, my heart broken for her pain and the pain that lay ahead, she awoke. Without a word, she got up on her knees and placed those scarred little hands on the stainless steel bars of the crib. Then she put her little scarred cheeks up against the rail and puckered her lips for a kiss. I've never heard a sermon so eloquent, nor heard the voice of the Holy Spirit so clearly. That night, I removed the little white glove from my briefcase and threw it away.

Chapter
Thirty-One

Furthermore we have had fathers of our flesh which corrected
us, and we gave them reverence: shall we not much rather be in
subjection unto the Father of spirits, and live? For they verily for
a few days chastened us after their own pleasure; but he for our
profit, that we might be partakers of his holiness.

Hebrews 12:9–10

This story is not simply the story
of a fire, of a mother, or of a little girl. In many ways, Becky's story
is still untold. There are so many choices yet to make, so many options
ahead. It's not just the story of a marriage, though because of this
fire, our marriage is something far different than it would have been
without it. It is more accurately the story of a message, a message
that has become a ministry. From it has grown the ministry of a
church and an unusual school God has raised up from the ashes—
the ministry of a family and a church they love and that loves them.
The struggles continue.

Hard lessons learned are valuable lessons, and those who appreciate them most have learned them firsthand. When people learn
about the fire, or hear the things we share about it, they sometimes
graciously give us credit for knowing things we do not yet know, for
having learned things we have not yet learned, for a maturity we do
not yet possess. There is a special kind of pressure that goes with that

responsibility. It is the pressure of feeling like a phony, of having credibility that you don't deserve.

There's also the pressure of exercising patience when someone
glibly says, "You just don't understand!" when we know it is they
who do not understand. But then we are learning that maybe we do
not, after all, understand. Having survived a heartache of our own
does not necessarily give us the empathy we need for others. There
is still that constant struggle with the pride of our human hearts. We
don't comfort others with our own strength just because we have
been comforted. If we comfort others at all, we do it with "the comfort wherewith we ourselves [have been] comforted" (2 Cor. 1:4).
Our encouragement for them is not our own to give, anymore than
the salvation we preach is not our salvation, but God's.

Faith is hopeful, it is not wishful thinking. In His Word God has
given us a book of answers; the problems of life will furnish the questions. Those who think it is always a cheap and easy task to learn the
answers to the questions have a shallow relationship with God.

Once a young Christian was pressing me to believe God wanted
to heal Becky.

"He has healed her," I replied.

"No, I mean really heal her," he insisted.

I just looked at him.

"If you had the faith, you could pray and God would make her
just like she was before the fire."

"Okay, maybe I'm weak," I said. "How about this? *You* pray and
ask God to make her like she was before."

That was the end of the conversation. The sad part was that he
still didn't get it.

Since our fire in 1978, thousands of other fires have taken place
and thousands of children have been burned. Many have died. Hundreds of times over the years, we have started to write this story, only
to realize that until we understood our experiences, we were dealing with the merely sensational, not the truly significant.

Even now, we admit that we do not fully understand the significance of these events. However, enough lessons are being learned
and enough opportunities to share them are occurring, that to keep
the experiences to ourselves would be one of the greatest tragedies
of all. And here perhaps comes one of the most significant lessons of

all: This really isn't the story of a tragedy; it's the story of a treasure—a treasure that might never have been found except through the purging fires of this experience.

* * *

In 1983, when Becky was seven years old, my mother almost died from a ruptured aneurysm. She came to live in our home and was with us for eight years. During that time she was dependent on us, and we had to care for her even though Becky was still very limited. The ministry was growing tremendously, and we had two more children.

God's grace was so real during those years. The truth that we comfort others with "the comfort wherewith we ourselves [have been] comforted" became the basic principle of my relationship with Mom. I was able to learn to be the kind of daughter God wanted me to be after I realized that God had given me the mother he wanted me to have.

When Mom had been with us for a few years, John made contact with Captain Butler, the man who had led Mom to the Lord nearly thirty years before. He had retired as a major in the Salvation Army and was still preaching revival meetings. John arranged for him to come to Greenville and see Mom on a surprise visit. It was a great reunion, and during that day John and I were assured of Mom's salvation.

As Captain Butler reminded Mom of her faith in Christ many years ago, she expressed her doubts. "But God couldn't forgive me after all I've done."

"Wilma, God forgave you the day you trusted Christ. He died for you two thousand years before you ever sinned the first time." And in the simple language that everyone in the hills of Kentucky had understood so well he added, "If God can make a lily grow in a hog pen so it smells like a lily instead of a hog, He can make your life what it ought to be—even now."

We rejoice at the true miracles God is working in our lives. We don't often see the kind of make-believe miracles shallow television evangelists portray or that many Christians still believe happen to others. But our family has seen resolution and forgiveness, and God has forgiven me. Both of those things are miracles.

I grieve when I hear all this popular talk about pressing charges against a loved one after twenty or thirty years—when a miracle-working counselor suddenly helps his counselee remember that abuse of long ago. The real tragedy is not that the abuse has ruined so much of their lives, but that their choice to get even or to get revenge is dooming the rest of their lives to bitterness.

We wept all the way through a book about a little boy who was burned a few years after Becky and I. His father had tried to kill him. How tragic! Yet more tragically, he seemed to be growing bitter. I heard him say on a talk show, "I hate my father." Yes, it is horrible that his body should be scarred, but more horrible that his soul should be scarred.

Over and over I have thought, *"Though I give my body to be burned, and have not love, it profiteth me nothing."*

* * *

In 1981, Becky was old enough to go to school, but there was no way she could handle it physically. Even if there had been a school available in which we could enroll her, her studies would have been interrupted several times each year, often for a month at a time, as she had to return to Cincinnati for additional surgery. I talked to every Christian school administrator in our area and looked at the public schools. Nothing was appropriate for Becky's needs. With our responsibilities at home and at church, there was no way I could teach her myself. We didn't know what to do.

Within a year after our family was back together, the Lord had blessed our home with another child, Daniel, for whom Becky had prayed. He was the most active child we had. Without Betty's help, Brenda couldn't have cared for him, much less teach Becky.

Then the Lord sent Bill Maher into our lives. Tom Harper introduced me to Bill, an evangelist who had been in the ministry for nearly thirty years. But there was something else about him that made him uniquely qualified to help us at this critical time. Bill had not walked until he was eleven years old nor used his hands until he was a teenager. As a child, Bill had suffered a severe case of cerebral palsy. But his parents wouldn't let him be an invalid. By the grace of God, he overcame his handicaps and gave his life to the Lord. Not only had he preached in evangelistic meetings all this time, but in his slurred and difficult speech he had preached on the radio for over twenty years. I knew I had to meet him. I scheduled him to come and preach at our church.

We hit it off immediately. Bill taught me how to look beyond the handicaps, how to spend enough time with people who are afflicted to get beyond the affliction, and how to love them for who they really are.

"Bill, how did you deal with your speech impediment when God called you to preach?" I asked.

"Well," he said, "I thought about Moses. He told God he couldn't go because he had a slow tongue. I knew if God was really calling me, He wouldn't let me out of it just because of that. I visited my preacher and told him I thought that God had called me to be a Baptist preacher, but I didn't know what to do about my speech impediment. He advised me to practice speaking like the famous Greek orator who put rocks in his mouth and practiced speaking. The preacher told me to put a handful of marbles in my mouth and just keep talking. Every day I would get rid of one of the marbles and, sure enough, when I lost all my marbles, I became a Baptist preacher." Bill broke into raucous laughter, slapping his knee and poking me in the ribs.

In the years ahead, I wondered if Bill was ever serious. He taught us something we knew intuitively, but that he had learned by experience. His ministry, God's Handi-work, was built on the principle that the afflicted have a responsibility to take the initiative, to use their disability to glorify the Lord. His message was strong and clear: "The disabled have no right to take advantage of their handicap for selfish purposes; it is a trust from God. This message makes no sense in the temporal world, but it is a treasure in the context of eternity."

Bill always made the first move. One night he and I were sitting on the platform. Just before Bill got up to preach, he walked down and pulled up the pants leg of a young fellow sitting on the front row. He was wearing black and red checkered socks. Bill pointed to them and said, "And you people think I'm afflicted!" Then came the booming laugh. The church fell in love with him.

Near the end of his meeting with us, I poured my heart out to him about not being able to find a place to put Becky in school. Without batting an eye, he stated, "You'll have to start a school."

"Sure," I said, "that's all I need."

"I'm serious," he responded.

"So am I," I replied.

"Why do you think God put you in this position?"

I didn't answer.

"You've got to start a school. Do you think Becky is the only child like this? I had to go to a school for the deaf because it was the only place that would take handicapped people. Have you ever heard of the Bill Rice Ranch?"

"Yes, we've been there. My wife spoke there once."

"Then you know how it got started," he said. "That's how God does these things. How do you think I started my ministry?"

"But, Bill, I don't know anything about starting a school. I've got my hands full trying to pastor this church."

"You don't need to know how to do it," Bill said. "Just obey the Lord. You know why you have to, and if you know why you have to do something, you'll always find out how to do it. Right?"

"Yeah, right, I guess," I said hesitantly.

"Okay, then, start a school."

"Just start a school," I uttered, "just like that."

"You got a better idea?" he asked.

We were both silent for a long time as Bill waited for me to reply. "You're not getting out of this one, boy," he declared as he roared with laughter.

Chapter
Thirty-Two

Now no chastening for the present seemeth to be joyous, but grievous: nevertheless afterward it yieldeth the peaceable fruit of righteousness unto them which are exercised thereby.

Hebrews 12:11

So we started a school. That fall Becky and Naomi, a young girl with Down syndrome, comprised our student body. The wife of the man who was helping with our Spanish church was our teacher. We had prayer, we said the Pledge. We had no idea what we were doing, but we did our best. Naomi and Becky encouraged each other. Naomi colored a lot of pictures, and Becky learned to hold a crayon between her hands. She learned her ABC's as we taped them in six-foot letters on the floor so she could trace them while walking with her walker.

I began to "beat the drum" for Christian special education. I studied books, attended conventions, and finally found a special education teacher. We held a kindergarten graduation that year. Becky pushed her little walker down the aisle in her white cap and gown to get her diploma. Hidden Treasure Christian School had begun!

The following year, our school had four students, and the next year twelve. It has grown each year since, and God has blessed it greatly. Today an excellent staff of special education professionals minister to children with a wide range of disabilities—physical, mental, and various learning disabilities. Though the educational needs of the students vary greatly, the spiritual needs are the same. We have tried to share with each student the principles God has made so clear to us. Many students have been greatly helped, both academically and spiritually. Quite a few have accepted the Lord as their personal Savior.

Through the influence of Hidden Treasure, many other Christian schools have started special education programs. Our staff wrote a reference book on Christian special education. Several Christian colleges now offer a major in special education. As I write, Becky will soon finish high school at Hidden Treasure Christian School.

By the school's third year, I was traveling widely, promoting the school, and raising support. Faith Baptist Church had moved to a new auditorium, and the multiple services were over. God had also sent us another son, Joseph.

Then I received a call from a missionary family in Texas. There was an eleven-year-old boy in the Rio Grande Children's Home named Marco Lopez. A missionary had found him begging on the streets in Guatemala. The missionary had brought him to the States for medical treatment, but the missionary had died. Marco still needed medical treatment. He had never been to school. He couldn't read or write, but he was a sweet boy. They wondered if we could take him in our school.

Where would he live? I wondered. *How could we support him?* "What is his problem?" I inquired.

"He was burned," the missionary said.

"How badly?" I probed.

"His face is badly scarred, and he has no hands."

"How was he burned?" I asked.

"A gasoline fire when he was two years old."

What could we do to help the boy? We were just getting started. There were so many challenges, so many kids needing our help. As I wondered what to say, the woman added, "I just know that your school is where Marco needs to be."

"We'll pray about it. Send me some information on him. I'll send you the application papers and see what we can do." Marco had no income, and for quite some time had not been in touch with his parents in Guatemala.

While speaking at a church near Northland Baptist Camp in Dunbar, Wisconsin, I shared the burden about Marco. A dear woman wrote me a check for his first year's tuition and room and board. I called the orphanage in Texas, and the missionary family made arrangements to bring him to Greenville. That same summer, Bill Maher introduced us to a family that kept handicapped foster children in Ohio and wanted to be involved in a ministry. They relocated to Greenville to help us with Hidden Treasure Christian School. Marco moved in with them. He would live there for the next five years.

Marco was a precious little boy, full of energy and excited about life. He learned English quickly. Later, he lived in our home for nearly two years after our boarding parents relocated. He was fitted with an artificial hand, and learned to read and write. When Becky went to Cincinnati for surgery, Marco accompanied us. He was the first of scores of children with no other place to turn that God would send our way.

In 1991 Marco's visa could not be renewed, and he returned to Guatemala with other missionaries. His brother now attends a Bible school, and both his parents have been saved. He calls us once a month.

The church was growing, the school was expanding, and our family was getting bigger. The whole ministry was expanding because the message was spreading. "We have this treasure in earthen vessels . . . we have everything we need to do God's will for our lives." Over and over we taught this message and shared it with others. God had given us a nationwide ministry with the handicapped. We would never have chosen it had God not thrust it upon us, but we would never give it up now for any price.

Survival stories offer tremendous encouragement to those seeking to survive. But after the crisis, we must learn to live in the routine of daily life—the often mundane circumstances where we so easily yield to the temptation to forget the lessons we have been learning. In a way, it's easy to trust the Lord in a crisis, to pray fervently that He will use us when we come face-to-face with the brevity of our lives. Sometimes the lessons of the crisis are lost in the daily grind. Sometimes they are hard to apply even when remembered.

It takes a long time for concepts to become convictions and longer still for our convictions to become our character, but we can still be thankful God never gives up on us. For those of us who have put our faith in Him, a work has begun that He will complete. All of us will be used in one way or another, as good examples or as bad ones. Someone once said that people either serve the Lord with their lives or complain about the service of others. Maybe those are our only options—to serve or be served. It seems that those who want only to be served are never satisfied. Until we are willing to comfort others with "the comfort wherewith we ourselves are comforted of God," we are not likely to rejoice in tribulation.

Trials don't make us—they reveal us. We must admit what we are so God can make us what He wants us to be. Not everyone will experience a painful physical trial, but all behavior will be purified in the way that God has planned for each of us. He knows what we need. He will do what's best.

In ours and others' trials, we are seeing another sobering truth. These experiences don't necessarily make us better; they can make us bitter. If we remain unbroken and refuse to see God's love behind the smelting process, we will become one of His bad examples.

Once-and-for-all lessons are as rare as once-and-for-all decisions. If either of these last, it is because those lessons are reviewed and reinforced just as those decisions are renewed again and again. Every time there is a temptation to go back on a commitment, we face the crisis again. Just as it gets easier to sin with repeated wrong decisions, it gets easier to have victory with repeated right choices.

If our family stays faithful to the Lord, it won't be because of the fire, or even what we have learned from the fire—it will be because God's grace is given anew each day. Truly we can rejoice in the truth of the verses Brenda has posted above our kitchen stove:

It is of the LORD's mercies that we are not consumed, because his compassions fail not. They are new every morning: great is thy faithfulness.

Lamentations 3:22–23

We frequently hear questions that show how wrong the world's concept of God really is: "How could God let this happen?" "How can you say that God is involved and then believe that He would not have prevented this tragedy?" We grieve with Him at our human stubbornness.

Sometimes men see God as a genie who appears at our command, grants our wishes, and disappears until we need Him again. This carnal view, like those selfish questions, reveals the impurity of belief in Christians as well as the unbelief of the world. But, God's faithfulness to us is great, though our faith toward Him is so small.

Just as my friend Bill struggled with cerebral palsy, so does the church struggle today. Even Christ's body is handicapped. Bill's limbs and members would not follow the commands and impulses of his brain, just as the members of the body of Christ often do not respond to the mind of Christ. The spastic and clumsy movements of the church throughout society bring sympathy and sarcasm from those who see the spectacle.

Perhaps what all of us need is to put our problems in perspective: to get a problem that is serious enough to bring us to our knees, to force us to overcome our flesh, to get our eyes off the earthen vessel and onto the treasure within.

Friends often ask us how all of this process of being broken by the Lord has affected our children. The answer is that they too have had the opportunity to be broken. Debbie had a struggle in her teenage years with doubts and bitterness. At fifteen, she fully dedicated her heart to the Lord during summer camp at the Wilds and has grown into a fine, beautiful young woman. She earned a master's degree from Bob Jones University in guidance and counseling and now works at Hidden Treasure Christian School.

John was only seven when the fire changed our lives; we had known much instability through our struggle up to that time. After the fire, so much attention was focused on Becky and the ministry that John seemed often to have to fend for himself. He is a tall, handsome man with a tender heart who is finding stability and structure for his life as a paratrooper with the 82nd Airborne. His little brothers and Becky look up to him with respect.

On Father's Day, 1982, Becky pushed her little walker down the aisle of our church to trust Christ as her personal Savior. She asked her daddy to share that experience in a gospel tract that has gone into over half a million hands so far. On Father's Day, 1992, she again came down the aisle to dedicate her life fully to the Lord's service. When she graduates from Hidden Treasure Christian School, she wants to attend a Christian college and prepare to write Christian books for teenagers.

* * *

One of the more difficult lessons our family has been learning is the fine art of dealing with people who have never been forced to understand that handicapped people are just regular people with special difficulties. With lots of practice at this task, Becky has developed a rather dry sense of humor and can often respond better than we can.

Not too long ago, Becky went with me to a speaking engagement. After the meeting, we were at a local restaurant. A woman came around a corner and bumped into us as we waited in line to order. Not realizing that Becky was a teenage girl in a wheelchair, the woman began to gush and coo and fuss over her, as one would a small baby, until everyone within hearing distance was thoroughly embarrassed. With a final pat and tweak, the woman left as abruptly as she'd come.

A thick silence reigned until Becky snapped the tension with a single sentence. "Well," she said. "Wasn't that special!"

We hadn't anticipated the pregnancy that occurred about six months after my release from the hospital. I was concerned that having more children would prevent me from giving Becky the care she needed. Now I realize that I probably would have made Becky an invalid by constant fussing. The Lord knew she needed to learn to do as much as possible for herself.

Daniel was less than two when Becky began praying for a baby sister.

"Well, just keep praying," I told her.

John gave me a leveling look. "You know you don't have any intentions of having any more," he said. Although Daniel was very gifted, he had been a challenge. He didn't sleep much, and he required a lot of care.

Shortly thereafter, I discovered that Joseph was on the way. However, we didn't know it was a boy. I thought the Lord was answering Becky's prayer for a baby sister. We let her pick out the name, and she chose "Mary." We had the name "Joseph Carroll" in reserve; it had been John's grandfather's name. I've always thought it was too bad we didn't have twins. We could have named them Joseph and Mary.

We were surprised when the doctor told us it was a boy, and we were a bit concerned about Becky's reaction. She thought about it for a few minutes. "He's pretty cute, Mom. Let's keep him."

* * *

Daniel was God's gift to Becky. More than anyone he has kept her from becoming dependent on others. Daniel was God's surprise to his mom and dad in answer to Becky's prayers. Without him we would not have been able to get back to normal when we did. Since he has never seen Becky or his mother without scars, Daniel helps us remember that ultimately scars don't matter. He is very protective of them both. As the most affectionate member of our family, he makes sure everyone gets plenty of hugs.

Joseph is the crown of our family. He's a soulwinner who will drop everything to talk to a neighbor about the Lord. He's a boy who, like his brother, John, has a tender heart and who, like his father, needs to know why. Joseph collects all the lessons that the rest of the family are learning and teaches them to us in a way we can understand.

One day in family devotions I was talking about love and lust. I asked Joe to explain the difference.

"Well, lust is wanting to get something for nothing," our nine-year-old son said. "And love is wanting to give something for nothing."

That is the answer, isn't it? And it is more precious than gold: giving something for nothing. Giving to get is only a medium of exchange—the simple currency of human relationships. But this gold is precious. It has value within itself. It must be tried and refined, but its value increases as it is purged and made pure. It is the price Jesus paid when He died on the cross. It is the price that God the Father paid when He gave up His only Son to die in our place.

It was a choice that even God Himself made: a choice to give something for nothing. We all have some choices to make in life: faith or fear, trust or lust, gold or glitter. God has been helping us to know that the choices must be made, and He has helped us learn some principles for making the right ones.

One principle is that you don't always make right choices but you can always make your choices right. You don't know the future and you might choose poorly, but you can always accept responsibility and try to correct your mistakes.

In our school for special children we teach the lessons God has been teaching us. In our book on special education, we deal at length with the biblical answer to emotional problems. The answer of course is to be found, as always, in personal responsibility—through obeying God by correcting the behavior causing the painful emotions.

In our ministry, we must testify of these lessons, and of course, we learn them more deeply as the war against the flesh continues. We can do things contrary to the will of God, but nothing can happen to us contrary to the will of God. We have everything we need to do God's will for our lives. A handicap is an exclamation point in your life's message. However it is said, the principle is the same. *Personal responsibility in submission to a sovereign God is more precious than gold.*

The words of Ron Hamilton's song express it eloquently:

God never moves without purpose or plan
When trying His servant and molding a man.
Give thanks to the Lord though your testing seems long;
In darkness He giveth a song.

I could not see through the shadows ahead;
So I looked at the cross of my Savior instead.
I bowed to the will of the Master that day;
Then peace came and tears fled away.

Now I can see testing comes from above;
God strengthens His children and purges in love.
My Father knows best, and I trust in His care;
Through purging more fruit I will bear.

O rejoice in the Lord. He makes no mistake.
He knoweth the end of each path that I take.
For when I am tried and purified,
I shall come forth as gold.[1]

There is still much dross in our lives, and the temptation even now is to lay this story aside for a few more years with the hope that some day we will be mature enough to share it with others. But we send it forth knowing that God will not be finished with us in this life. We won't truly come forth as gold until we have gone through the final trial.

Christ taught us that "the pure in heart . . . shall see God." The pure in heart are not the righteous. The term Christ used means pure in substance, uncorrupted, unadulterated. Instability of life is the fruit of doublemindedness—wanting our way while experimenting with God's way. When we have become singleminded about our dedication to God, we recognize Him in every circumstance. Our prayer for ourselves and for our readers is that we will continue to become pure in heart until we see Him face to face—that we will all come to know what is truly more precious than gold.

Epilogue

A Word
from Becky

My earliest memory is of the hospital—not the first time I was there, but later. I'm thankful I don't remember the fire. It used to scare me when I would hear Mom and Dad talk about it. It scares me now to go back to the hospital. I have had surgery fifty-seven times. I'm glad for everything the doctors have done for me, and I know that there are some things they can't do. I wish I could walk by myself. I wish I could see out of my right eye. I wish my hands were stronger. But I'm glad I made it, and I'm glad for my family and friends.

God has been very good to me. I have had 171 blood transfusions, and I don't have AIDS. I have a school across the street from my house that my Dad started. I have teachers that understand me and friends that like me for who I am. I like it best when people just treat me like a person. I know I was burned, but I don't want to be called a "victim." Several years ago I asked my Dad to write a tract that I could give to people who stared at me in public. I was saved when I was six years old, and I know that without the Lord's help I couldn't face the struggles I live with every day. I wouldn't be honest if I said I was glad for all I have been through or that I didn't want to be able to live a normal life. But really, I've never known any-thing else. I want to use my life for the Lord. One summer at camp I rededicated my life to Him. When I graduate from high school next year, I hope I can go to a Christian college.

This is Mom and Dad's story. I don't mind that they told some things about me, because I know they are trying to help others. But I'm glad they are going to let me tell my own story myself. I'm not sure what that story will be yet. I'm seventeen. I have a lot of deci-sions to make in the future. Sometimes I go to meetings with my Mom. I'm proud of her—she saved my life—but I don't like to talk to groups. I'm too shy, I guess. I'm only telling you this because I'm writing it and you're not looking at me.

I know there are lots of other girls who feel like I do. They think they are ugly sometimes. They think no one likes them. I know that boys are sometimes interested only in how we look. But I'm learn-ing what is really important in life. We are just here for a little while, but we will be in heaven forever. Long after I have a perfect body, others will just be starting to know the kind of suffering I have behind me—only theirs will be forever.

There have been lots of letters from people who have been saved and who have read our tract. I pray that lots of others will be helped by this book.

More people have prayed for me than I have even met. I am thank-ful for those prayers and those people. I know that God loves me. I know that Mom and Dad love me. We're not perfect . . . but we're working on it.

I'm glad I'm alive.

Rebecca Morel Vaughn
May 1993

Rejoice In The Lord

Ron Hamilton   Ron Hamilton

1. God nev-er moves with-out pur-pose or plan When
2. I could not see through the shad-ows a-head; So I
3. Now I can see test-ing comes from a-bove; God

try-ing His ser-vant and mold-ing a man.___ Give
looked at the cross of my Sav-ior in-stead.___ I
strength-ens His chil-dren and purg-es in love.___ My

thanks to the Lord though your test-ing seems long; In
bowed to the will of the Mas-ter that day; Then
Fa-ther knows best, and I trust in His care; Through

dark-ness He giv-eth a song.___
peace came and tears fled a-way.___
purg-ing more fruit I will bear.___

Chorus

O re-joice in the Lord. He makes no mis-take. He___

know - eth the end of each path that I take. For when I am

tried and pur - i - fied, I shall come forth as gold.

Becky, age ten, and Ron "Patch the Pirate" Hamilton. Ron lost his eye to cancer the same week Becky was burned in 1978.

For more information on Patch the Pirate's music, contact: Majesty Music P.O. Box 66524 Greenville, SC 29606 803-242-6722

Notes

Preface

1. A. W. Tozer, *Renewed Day by Day: A Daily Devotional,* compiled by G. B. Smith (Camp Hill, Pa.: Christian Publications, 1980). Devotional for February 20.

Chapter Thirty-Two

1. Ron Hamilton, "Rejoice in the Lord" (© Majesty Music, 1978). Used by permission.

For a free copy of the gospel tract "Hidden Treasure," write:

Hidden Treasure
500 W. Lee Road
Taylors, SC 29687